The Quakers and the
English Revolution

The Quakers
and the
English Revolution

BARRY REAY

Foreword by Christopher Hill

St. Martin's Press
New York

All rights reserved. For information, write:
St. Martin's Press, Inc., 175 Fifth Avenue, New York, NY 10010.
Printed in Great Britain by The Camelot Press Ltd
First published in the United States of America in 1985

ISBN 0-312-65808-7

Library of Congress Cataloging in Publication Data

Reay, Barry.
   The Quakers and the English Revolution.

   Includes index.
   1. Society of Friends—England—History—17th century.
2. Great Britain—History—Puritan Revolution, 1642-1660.
3. England—Church history—17th century. I. Title.
BX7676.2.R4 1985   289.6'42   84-22355
ISBN 0-312-56808-7

CONTENTS

Foreword

During the present generation our understanding of the early history of the Quakers has been transformed. Thanks especially to theses and articles by Alan Cole and Barry Reay, we now know that for the first decade of their existence Quakers – with the exception of some individuals – were by no means pacifists. There is a natural tendency when writing the history of religious sects to read backwards, to push back into the seventeenth century the image of the sober, grey-clad, moderate, industrious and prospering Quakers which we know from the eighteenth century. This image has now been shattered for the first decade of Quaker history, and it is greatly to the credit of the *Journal of the Friends' Historical Society* that it has contributed its share to recovering the often bellicose radicalism of Quakers in the 1650s.

Before turning to the Quakers, Barry Reay had written a valuable study of the Muggletonians, another sect founded in the 1650s, and for long the Quakers' principal rival.[1] Being able to compare these two sects, later so very different, enabled him to understand the importance of the revolutionary ambiance in which they originated; and to appreciate the transformation which came over both sects in the later seventeenth century. In this book Barry Reay draws on a great deal of work, by himself and others, to give a new synthesis which makes sense both of the Quakers' early political radicalism and of the rethinking which took place after 1660.

But it is more than the early history of a sect, important though the Society of Friends is in the history of our civilization. Barry Reay's book offers a number of reinterpretations of English history which historians will have to think about. He suggests that the radical demands put forward by the Quakers, particularly their demand for the abolition of tithes, had a polarizing effect on society in the late 1650s. They outraged most

1 Reprinted as 'The Muggletonians: An Introductory Survey', in *The World of the Muggletonians* (by C. Hill, B. Reay and W. Lamont, 1983), pp. 23–63.

of the gentry, the clergy and traditionalists of all classes; they recalled the platform of the Levellers (suppressed in 1649) and of the True Levellers or Diggers (suppressed in 1650). Not only enemies of the Quakers denounced them as Levellers; a friend like George Wither said 'they are our Levellers new-named'.

Barry Reay suggests, with a great deal of supporting evidence drawn from a wide variety of printed and manuscript sources, that alarm at the extraordinarily rapid growth of the Quaker movement in the fifties contributed significantly to the shift in opinion which led to the restoration of Charles II in 1660 – much to the surprise of his royalist supporters. In 1659 there seemed a possibility that social controls might break down; that a desperate republican government might put arms into the hands of Quakers, Anabaptists and other radicals. Social revolution, averted in 1647-9, seemed to be looming again. The main emphasis in the propaganda of George Monck as he marched down to London from Scotland at the beginning of 1660 was the danger to society from 'fanaticks'.

We know that the threat never materialized; and the pacifism which the Quakers adopted after 1660 makes it easy to dismiss it as the creation of hysterical fears. This is the sort of hindsight to which those historians are especially prone who think that the rule of the gentry was somehow 'normal' and that the radicals were an insignificant minority. Dr Reay's careful and well-documented argument shows that we must think again. If he is right, as I think he is, his title suggests that we may also have to reassess the importance of radical ideas and groupings in the English Revolution as a whole.

Christopher Hill

For my parents
Gladys and Kenneth Reay

Preface

I began work on this book rather a long time ago, and over the years I have incurred a number of debts. The editors of *History* and *Social History* have permitted me to use and revise material which originally appeared in those journals. Oxford University Press gave me an opportunity to re-formulate some of my ideas, and air them in a short essay on the Quakers in a volume edited by J. F. McGregor and myself. Freda Christie typed and retyped the manuscript, often under conditions of extreme provocation. Hugh Jackson kindly read what I had thought was the finished product and provided me with some cogent and constructive criticism. Philip Almond, Paul Baker, Robert Dare, Colin Davis, Austin Gough, Günther Kress, William Lamont, Frank McGregor, John Morrill, Mike Presdee, Wilfrid Prest, and Keith Thomas have been helpful in a variety of ways at different stages. The staffs of the Bodleian, British, Friends House, Dr Williams's, and Worcester College Libraries have given me a great deal of assistance; as have archivists and their assistants at the Public, Bristol, Cambridgeshire, Cheshire, Chester, Cornwall, Cumbria, Devon, Dorset, Essex, Hampshire, Hertfordshire, Kent, Norfolk, Somerset, East and West Sussex, and Wiltshire record offices. Friends Historical Library, Dublin, the Historical Society of Pennsylvania, and the Mount School, York, kindly supplied me with xeroxes of much-needed material. Joan Law of the University of Auckland Library has been extremely helpful in procuring microfilms from overseas. And of course none of my research would have been possible without the support provided by the various institutions which have sheltered me over the years: the University of Adelaide, Balliol College, Hartley College of Advanced Education, and my present home the University of Auckland.

But I have two great debts. The first is to my family, Athina,

Preface

Kristina, and Alexa, for their encouragement, support, and forbearance, and to my mother and father for their enthusiasm. My other debt is to Christopher Hill, who for some ten years has gently nurtured this project.

University of Auckland, 1984

And now is the seperation, the sheep from the goats, the wheat from the tares, and Christ is come to set at varience father against son, and son against father, and wife against the man, and the man against the wife, and to turn the world upside downe; and this is the cause why the world rages.

J. Parnell, *A Shield of the Truth* (1655)

Introduction

This book is about the early Quakers (the Society of Friends), but it is also about the English Revolution and popular thought and activity. Thus I have had several aims in writing it. Like Christopher Hill's account of radical ideas during the English Revolution, or J. F. C. Harrison's examination of popular millenarianism in the eighteenth and nineteenth centuries, it is, in part, an essay in popular history.[1] It is, I hope, a contribution towards the quest for a 'history of the inarticulate', 'history from below'. It was in fact this aspect of early Quakerism which initially attracted my interest. As anyone familiar with the work of Christopher Hill and A. L. Morton now knows, the English Revolution was a time of unprecedented radical activity and openness when ordinary women and men discussed, debated, and fought for notions and ideals that have yet to be realized. If it is to the *sans-culottes*, the *Enragés* and Gracchus Babeuf that we have to look for the radical wing of the French Revolution, it is to the sectarian milieu that we must look for radical activity during the English upheaval, for in the seventeenth century most popular political and social protest was expressed in religious terms. The Quakers were a product of this milieu. They represent one of the 'attempts of various groups of the common people to impose their own solutions to the problems of their time',[2] and as such surely deserve our attention. So to some extent my interest lies not with the Quaker movement *per se* but with what the movement tells us about the hopes and fears of ordinary people during the seventeenth century.

This book is also an attempt to bring some social and political history into the sometimes staid and insular field of religious history. As protest movements, sects can inform us not only about themselves but about the society which they are rejecting. And the way in which a society treats its dissidents can, after all, tell us much about that society. So, in a sense, the Quakers can be seen as a sort of foil by means of which it is possible to ask all kinds of questions about seventeenth-century society. Through Quakerism we can enter the world of the 'subordinate classes' from two directions. The Quakers are important as a concrete example of popular aspirations and discontent. But they are also interesting in that they were the objects of a considerable amount of hostility from people of the same sections of society. The 'middling' and 'poorer sort of people' not only joined and showed support for the Quakers, they (though obviously not the same individuals) also attacked them. Thus Quakerism has potential for telling us something about what has sometimes been called the unacceptable side of popular activity: its xenophobic, parochial, deferential side. Finally, Quakerism allows us to approach the ruling classes, to use Jesse Lemisch's phrase, 'from the bottom up'. The Quakers clashed with the seventeenth-century elite, and the elite's response tells us something of their attitudes and fears as well as the operation of the state – how the ruling class ruled. So while this book concentrates on one sect – the Quakers – during a brief period of history – the 1650s – I am convinced that a single, detailed case study can shed light in many directions and illuminate a variety of important issues.

· Of course there is no shortage of studies of the early Quakers. Eduard Bernstein, for example, was interested in the socio-economic aspects of Quakerism, including two chapters on the movement in his *Sozialismus und Demokratie in der grossen Englischen Revolution* (translated into English in 1930 as *Cromwell and Communism*). There is W. C. Braithwaite's still formidable two-volume general history. More recently there has been some good work on the Quakers in various studies by Hugh Barbour, Alan Cole, Christopher Hill, J. F. Maclear, Keith Thomas, and Richard Vann.[3] Demographers have made use of the excellent Quaker registers, and we are apparently on the way towards a definitive history of the demography of English and Irish Quakers.[4] A historian of the family has looked to the sect (in late seventeenth-century Pennsylvania) for the origins of the modern American family: 'a basic source of American culture: the first scene of a major, widespread, obviously successful assertion of the child-centred, fond-fostering, nuclear family in early America and most likely in the Anglo-American world'.[5] Even an ethnographer of language has discovered the early

Friends, claiming them as folk precursors of the symbolic interactionists.[6]

Yet it would still be true to say that there is no short survey of early Quaker thought and behaviour, no short synthesis that takes into account recent studies of the movement. To a large extent we are still forced to see the Quakers through the spectacles of their latter-day co-religionists and sympathizers. Thus a concern with the spiritual rather than the social permeates the work of both Geoffrey Nuttall and Hugh Barbour. The former has obviously been attracted to seventeenth-century Quakerism because of his belief that its effusive spirit has much to offer current religious thought and theology, while Barbour was keen that his book *The Quakers in Puritan England* 'open the way for deeper discussions between liberal and conservative Quakers, as well as between Friends and non-Friends'.[7] When reading such work one could even be forgiven for forgetting that there was, after all, a revolution in the middle of the seventeenth century, and that the Quakers were a product of that revolution. In part, my book is a response to this state of affairs. It sets out to provide a brief account of early Quakerism, arguing that the movement was far more radical than some historians would still admit.

This book is also a response to what I perceive to be a major shortcoming in all studies of early Quakerism, the failure of its historians to make use of non-Quaker sources. This is unfortunate, for there is a wealth of seventeenth-century materials: state papers, church court, quarter sessions, assize and Exchequer records, non-Quaker diaries and collections of correspondence, a mass of anti-Quaker literature. It is from this source material that it is possible to construct an account of what can be described as the other side of the coin of Quakerism: the image of the early movement, how Quakers were perceived by their contemporaries; their actual impact on seventeenth-century politics and society.

This book, then, is not an attempt to replace the work of Hugh Barbour or W. C. Braithwaite; it aims rather to provide an added dimension to Quaker studies. I believe that just as Eugene Genovese has argued that it is impossible to write a history of slaves without a history of their masters, it is meaningless to write a history of Quakers without taking into account their relationship with contemporaries. The book begins with an account of early Quaker ideology and activity, discussing the movement's social and ideological origins, its emergence during the Interregnum and its rapid growth as the most radical and successful of the Revolution sects. The next section (Part 2) deals with responses to the Quakers – those of the authorities and the elite as well as those of the general populace – and suggests that the predominant reaction was one of fear and hostility. Part 3, the core of the book, develops some of the themes implicit in the preceding sections. The argument is that fear and hatred of Quakers, as part of a more general fear of sectaries, had its political repercussions, contributing in 1659-60 to the reaction which ended in the restoration of Charles II. Just as fear of social revolution had galvanized support for the King's party in the 1640s during the early years of civil war,[8] it led many in 1659, particularly the gentry, to look to the monarchy as the only salvation from social anarchy. Finally, Part 4 examines the more conservative path that Quakerism took after 1660, charting the course of that change and asking why it was that Quakerism underwent such a rapid transformation.

PART I   DIMENSIONS

CHAPTER 1

Birth of a movement

I

Histories of the seventeenth-century Quakers traditionally begin with the early life of George Fox, a shoemaker's apprentice from Leicestershire and the acknowledged founder of the movement, who left home in the 1640s to wander around the Midlands. Fox travelled south, as far as London, suffering the usual Puritan doubts and despairs and discoursing on spiritual matters with a variety of people. He met those 'that held women have no souls . . . no more than a goose', and others who 'relied much on dreams'.[1] Eventually, in 1647, at the age of twenty-three, he found enlightenment. The 'Lord opened unto me that being bred at Oxford or Cambridge was not enough to fit and qualify men to be ministers of Christ'. Church-going was unimportant because God dwelled in men's and women's hearts; the church 'was noe more holy then another peice of Grounde'.[2] By 'his immediate Spirit and power', God revealed to Fox that 'every man was enlightened by the divine light of Christ . . . and that they that believed in it came out of condemnation and came to the light of life and became the children of it' and that 'such as were faithful to him in the power and light of Christ, should come up into that state in which Adam was before he fell'.[3] The emphasis was on the light or spirit within. It led to salvation, and, as we shall see later, to perfection. It gave new knowledge: 'The creation was opened to me', wrote Fox, 'and it was showed me how all things had their names given them according to their nature and virtue. And I was at a stand in my mind whether I should practise physic for the good of mankind, seeing the nature and virtues of the creatures were so opened to me by the Lord.'[4] Fox claimed to be able to 'discern the spirits' within those he met, since the 'spiritual man discerns and Judgeth all things'.[5] The spirit was above the Scriptures. It 'is not the Scriptures' which are to be the touchstone of truth, Fox asserted, it is 'the Holy Spirit, by which the holy men of God gave forth the Scriptures, whereby opinions, religions, and judgements were to be tried'.[6]

In 1647 or 1648 Fox was living in the Mansfield area, presumably working as a shoemaker. For the next four years he travelled around the Midlands and Yorkshire; suffering imprisonment in 1650 on a charge of blasphemy; establishing contacts with pockets of separatists near Doncaster and Wakefield who had clearly reached the Quaker position independently of Fox, enthusiasts who 'met in silent meetings, with fasting and prayer, waiting upon the Lord'.[7] By 1652 Fox and fellow itinerants – Richard Farnworth, Thomas Aldam, Margaret Killam, William Dewsbury, and James Nayler – were moving through the rural areas of northern England, linking together groups of separatists. This, and not the early activity of Fox, marks the beginning of the Quaker movement.

This is not to deny Fox's importance, his influence, or his undoubted charisma. It is rather to make Richard Vann's point that in the 1650s it was by no means clear that Fox, as his sectarian rival Lodowick Muggleton might have put it, was going to be the 'longest liver'.[8] There were, and would be, others upon whom the mantle of 'founder' could have fallen, others who had already established their own divine commissions. Nayler was to record his in 1653, in Westmorland, in an Appleby court: 'I was at the plough, meditating on the things of God, and suddenly I heard a Voice, saying unto me, "Get thee out from thy kindred and from thy father's house". And I had a promise given in with it. Whereupon I did exceedingly rejoice, that I had heard the Voice of that God which I had professed from a child, but had never known him.' There was, as W. C. Braithwaite correctly notes, no special reference to Fox.[9] Fox's powerful *Journal* dominates our view of early Quakerism: we tend to see things through Fox's eyes. Yet if we think ourselves into the 1650s we find Nayler, Farnworth, Dewsbury, Richard Hubberthorne, Edward Burrough, any of whom were then as important or influential as Fox. When two Kendal Quakers were detained in Beverley in 1653 for selling and reading from 'scurulous & scandalous' pamphlets, the literature seized was by Nayler, Farnworth, and John Harwood.[10] And if we were to concentrate on the political impact of the Quaker movement during the Interregnum, the crucial names would be Hubberthorne, Burrough, George Fox the younger, and George Bishop: not that of George Fox.[11]

But most of these men would be dead a decade later. Fox lived on.

So the birth of the Quaker movement was less a gathering of eager proselytes at the feet of a charismatic prophet, than a linking of advanced Protestant separatists into a loose kind of church fellowship with a coherent ideology and a developing code of ethics. In 1652 and 1653, 'the People of God', 'Children of Light', or Quakers as they had become known – the movement appropriated a term first given in abuse[12] – continued their work in the North. These were the days of the silk and ribbon burning at Malton (Yorkshire), when shopkeepers testified against pride and extravagance, and when women left their husbands to serve the Lord.[13] When Farnworth spoke to a crowd at Wakefield market a captain's wife was much 'wrought on'; she cried out 'This is the power of the Lord' and proceeded to rip off her silver lace.[14] Quakers proclaimed their message in churches and churchyards, and pinned pamphlets to market crosses. In 1652 Fox also established important links with a group of separatists who were based near Kendal in Westmorland, but who lived in something like a seven-mile radius which encompassed villages in Yorkshire and Lancashire. The Kendal area provided many of the principal Quaker 'ministers' and pamphleteers of the 1650s: Francis Howgil and John Audland (lay preachers to the gathered churches in the region), Edward Burrough, John Camm, Richard Hubberthorne, and Ann Blaykling. By 1654 there were Quaker communities in all the northern counties, from Cheshire to Northumberland, as well as Fox's contacts in the Midlands whose exact status or condition at this time is unclear. The movement had also managed to establish bases under the protective wing of sympathetic or converted justices: Thomas Fell at Swarthmore in Lancashire; Gervase Benson at Sedbergh in Yorkshire; Anthony Pearson at Ramshaw in Durham.

The early 'converts' were for the most part ordinary men and women who had spurned the wishes of their betters and who had already rejected much of the ideology and organization of orthodox Puritanism. Many were engaged in some form of agricultural work, either as yeomen or husbandmen. It seems that several had been in conflict with landlords in the 1640s, over their opposition to excessive rents and manorial services.[15] Others had been refusing to pay tithes.[16] From the start, the Quaker movement was a movement of political and social as well as religious protest. Richard Baxter noted the youth of those attracted to Quakerism – 'young, raw professors and women, and ignorant, ungrounded people that were but novices and learners in the principles'.[17] We know the ages of some forty Quakers converted before 1654, mainly those of the so-called 'valiant sixty', the first adherents to Quakerism. The average age at conversion was twenty-eight, the mean was twenty-six. In other words, they were in their late teens during the civil war years, but would have had little experience of Charles I's personal rule. Some of the leading Quakers were indeed young. Edward Burrough and James Parnell turned Quaker at the ages of nineteen and sixteen respectively (Parnell was dead before he was twenty-one). But Hubberthorne was in his mid-twenties when he became a Quaker; Howgil, Audland, and Nayler were in their mid-thirties (they were adults when civil war began); Camm was in his forties; Elizabeth Hooton, whom we will encounter later, was fifty-one. The northern 'first publishers of truth', then, spanned several generations. Richard Vann's work on Buckinghamshire, Norwich, and Norfolk Quakers indicates that early conversions after the sect moved southwards in 1654 were, if anything, of people slightly older, with a median and an average age in the thirties.[18] Quakerism was by no means limited to the very young.

Quakerism began in the North. But it was not until 1654 and 1655, with the movement of Quaker preachers southwards, that the movement really made its impact. In the autumn of 1654 the sect made a dramatic appearance in London itself, with Camm, Burrough, and Hubberthorne reporting successes among groups of Seekers and Baptists, and meetings with Gerrard Winstanley the Digger leader, Joshua Sprigge, and Colonel Nathaniel Rich. The Quakers visited groups of Independents, and they encountered some people who were 'translating . . . the scriptures anew, and judges it by their reason'. Our 'noyse and fame is much spread in this City', wrote Burrough, and he mentioned that spies attended meetings and then reported back to Whitehall.[19] In the following year Nayler continued the work of Burrough and Hubberthorne, but this time there were links with groups of upper-class enthusiasts. Over the next few years the sect was to make inroads into well-known families.[20] By 1655 Quakerism was a national problem rather than a regional nuisance. For William Prynne the prediction of Jeremiah 1:14

had finally proved true: 'That out of THE NORTH AN EVILL SHALL BREAK FORTH UPON ALL THE INHABITANTS OF THE LAND'.[21]

The early years of 'the Quaker Awakening' were dramatic years, and their story has already been eloquently told.[22] It was a time of enthusiasm, of powerful preaching – on the moors, in fields and orchards, in prisons, from barns. In 1654 Quaker 'ministers' reported from Bristol that they were holding meetings each day; the house would fill, the street would fill, 'soe the voyce went forth for a feeld & we wente to it like an army'.[23] At a meeting in London, which lasted from 3 p.m. until midnight, a Quaker woman spoke 'untill her naturell brith was spent' and 'still did strive to speake'.[24] Quakers undertook gruelling itineraries in an effort to spread the word, first through Britain (from Land's End to the Orkneys), and then to France, the Palatinate, Holland, Denmark, Venice, Rome, Constantinople, Jerusalem, and to New England, Barbados, Jamaica, Surinam. Quaker pamphlets were produced in startling numbers: over 500 titles in the years 1653-7, another 500 from 1658 to 1660.[25]

The success of the movement was impressive. Within a decade there were certainly from 35,000 to 40,000 Quakers (men, women, and children), perhaps as many as 60,000. They were as numerous as Catholics, more numerous than either Fifth Monarchists or Baptists. As Hugh Barbour has suggested, it must at times have seemed as if the whole of England would turn Quaker.[26] Not one county escaped the effects of Quaker proselytizing. Nor, as we shall see, did Quakers concentrate on towns and cities; in fact in contrast with all the stereotypes of early nonconformity as an essentially *urban* affair, the indications are that although Bristol and London were important Quaker strongholds Quakerism was predominantly a rural movement. The Quakers, Bernard Capp has reminded us, demonstrated that sectarianism could flourish in the villages.[27] They were the most successful as well as the most radical of the Revolution sects.

Although in this volume I tend to use the terms interchangeably, Vann has argued that for Quakerism before 1670 the word 'movement' is more appropriate than 'sect'.[28] Organization in the early years was loose and informal, modelled almost certainly on that of the General Baptists[29] who provided the Quakers with so many of their early recruits. Local congregations scattered throughout the nation were linked by itinerant 'ministers'. In the late 1660s Fox was to reorganize the movement into a fully fledged sect with regular local, regional, and national meetings, and central control.[30] In the 1650s cohesion was provided by the travelling 'ministers' and by the occasional General Meeting where delegates from local areas would meet to co-ordinate campaigns – against tithes, for example – or to collect money to help with the spreading of 'Truth'.[31] Travelling Quakers of status – William Dewsbury was one of whom we know[32] – would sometimes adjudicate on matters of discipline, but there was nothing approaching the disciplinary system which came with the business meetings of the 1660s and 1670s. As we shall see, Quaker doctrine and practice were remarkably coherent, yet it is true to say that the situation in the 1650s allowed a fluidity and an extravagance not permitted even a decade later.[33]

II

As the Quakers themselves realized, England had a history of heresy and nonconformity which stretched back at least to the fourteenth century and which included groups such as the Lollards, Familists, and Anabaptists. The leaders of these groups and movements were often university men or members of the clergy. But the rank and file were mostly craftsmen and tradesmen, men (and their wives) who were sometimes, as in the case of the Lollards, closely linked to the highly mobile cloth and wool trade. In such cases economic and ideological interaction went hand in hand. Some of the themes of Lollardism anticipate those of the Protestant radicals. They were hostile to the magic and ceremony of the Catholic church, and rejected intermediaries (be they sacramental or priestly). Holy bread and holy water had no special properties. Christ's body was not present in the sacrament of the altar. Images should not be honoured and there was no point in praying to saints (devotion should be direct to God). Pilgrimages were of no value; it would be better to donate the potential expenses to the poor. Extreme unction was unnecessary, as was confession to a priest: 'God alone could forgive and remit sins'. Baptism and confirmation were also superfluous because people were 'baptized' and 'confirmed' by the Holy Spirit. Every believer, man or woman, was a priest. The Scriptures should be available in English so that they would be accessible to ordinary men and women. Strongest in Bristol, Coventry, the Thames valley, the Chilterns, London, Kent, and

East Anglia, Lollardism continued from the fourteenth to the sixteenth century, when it merged with the Protestantism of the Henrician Reformation.[34]

The fate of the English brand of the small spiritual movement called the Family of Love was much the same. It established roots in England in the mid-sixteenth century only to disappear in the seventeenth century amidst the ideological flux of the Revolution. By the 1640s Familism was a term 'vague enough to be all but totally meaningless'. We know less about the activities and beliefs of the Family of Love than we do about Lollardism. The writings of the movement's founder Henry Niclaes were in circulation in England in the 1570s, but his ideas were modified by indigenous heterodoxy. English Familists, who were to be found mainly in the Isle of Ely and East Anglia, seem to have believed that the spirit was above the Bible (although they were none the less saturated in its language), that it was possible to attain the perfection of Adam before the Fall and thus become free from sin, that Hell existed in the agony of this world, and that the Crucifixion, Resurrection, and Judgement were all internal spiritual stages on the road to perfection. Most of these ideas were taken up in the 1640s and 1650s by the Quakers and other sectaries.[35]

There were Anabaptists in England from the 1530s, although they are sometimes difficult to distinguish from the Lollards. The General (non-Calvinist) Baptists had come into being by 1612; by 1625 there were at least five congregations in various parts of the nation. They taught adult baptism, yet their most important tenet according to Murray Tolmie was the doctrine of 'general redemption', that it was possible for all to achieve salvation. Finally there was a group of separatists called the Jacob circle. Founded by Henry Jacob and based in London, this church foreshadowed the Independent movement of the 1640s: the individual congregation (in association with other congregations) as 'the true visible church'.[36]

But it was not until the 1640s, with the start of civil war, that separatism became a substantial movement. For the Quakers' arrival in the 1650s was but the latest in a whole line of radical groups, movements, and individuals produced during the turmoil of 1642-60: the Baptists, Calvinist and non-Calvinist, who practised adult baptism (by total immersion) and who provided many recruits for the Levellers and Quakers; the

Levellers, who emphasized what Richard Overton called 'Practical Christianity' – action against oppression in its various forms – and who pressed for democratic reform of parliament, the law, and local government, indeed for massive decentralization of political power; the Diggers, who advocated, and for a short term practised, agrarian communism, and whose spokesman, Gerrard Winstanley, has justly found an important place in the history of English political thought; the Ranters, who were probably never a coherent movement but rather a loose body of individuals who believed that to the pure all things are pure and that sin exists only in the imagination; the Fifth Monarchy Men, a pressure group who believed quite literally in a shortly expected millennium (the reign of Christ on Earth), a time of godly rule based on the laws of the Old Testament; the Seekers, who were not a movement in either the doctrinal or organizational sense but simply men and women who held that all church ordinances and rituals were invalid, and who awaited further divine guidance and revelation; and finally a miscellany of popular messiahs and prophets, those whom the prophet Lodowick Muggleton (co-founder of the Muggletonian sect) had heard in London in 1650, 'Christs and prophets and Virgin Maries and such-like', 'that were about the streets and declared the day of the Lord and many other wonderful things, as from the Lord'.[37]

However much historians may ponder the precise theological ancestry of Quakerism, it is clear that the movement itself was a product of the English Revolution. It is difficult to recapture the spirit of those years. By the time the Quakers had arrived on the scene at the beginning of the 1650s, the nation had been through two civil wars. A king and his archbishop of Canterbury had been tried and executed. The House of Lords, the institution of bishops, church courts, the Star Chamber and Court of High Commission, had been abolished. Censorship had ended – in fact, if not in theory. The Army had become a power broker, much in the way that it has in many Third World nations today; legislative assemblies were to arrive and depart according to the wishes of the military. The Rump Parliament, born of the Army's purge of the Long Parliament in December 1648, was sitting at Westminster when George Fox travelled towards the North of England in the winter of 1651 (the first stage in the founding of the Quaker movement). Thereafter the history of Interregnum

Quakerism coincides with what has been called 'the quest for settlement', when England's new rulers walked a political tightrope between the irreconcilable demands of radicals and conservatives: Barebone's Parliament of 1653 (the Parliament of Saints), Cromwellian Protectorate of 1653-9, the hectic changes in central power during 1659-60.

This is not the place to discuss the somewhat complicated ecclesiastical history of 1642-60, but it is possible to sketch a brief outline.[38] The Church of England was assaulted by statute. Ordinances ordered the demolition of Anglican church government and liturgy. But as John Morrill has shown, there was a gap between legislative intent and actual implementation. Anglicanism displayed a vast amount of resilience, and Presbyterianism was never successfully imposed upon the nation.[39] What existed, then, was a fairly broadly based church which permitted a wide range of opinions. One should not become too starry-eyed about the freedom of the 1640s and 1650s, however. Parliament could and did take action against radicals. 'Blasphemous and execrable' opinions were punished. Religious toleration was *de facto* rather than *de jure*; it frequently depended on the whims of the rulers of the local communities. Yet despite all the caveats that can be made, the single most important aspect of the religious history of this period is the shattering of both Puritanism and the Church of England, and the emergence of hundreds of independent and semi-independent congregations.

III

As far as the better-known Quakers are concerned (the 'ministers' and pamphlet writers), the influence of Puritanism is indisputable when one comes to consider the ideological roots of early Quakerism. Many Quakers, like Isaac Penington, had become 'exceedingly entangled' about Calvin's theory of predestination, 'having drunk in that doctrine, according as it was then held forth by the strictest of those that were termed Puritans'.[40] They were thoroughly imbued with the Puritan sense of sin; they despaired of their salvation. George Fox spent his pre-Quaker days sitting in hollow trees, and tobacco, psalm-singing and blood-letting were suggested to him as potential cures for his condition.[41] Before he became a Quaker, George Rofe was 'smot by the hand of the Lord into many fears of what should become of me hereafter, and have often wept exceedingly in secret and in my bed, so that I have wetted much clothes with teares'.[42] Quakerism saved John Crook from his fear of the Devil; 'I was so possessed with fear, that I looked behind me lest the Devil stood there to take me.'[43] We could go on: Quakerism was to some extent a reaction to this psychological malaise.

Several Quakers began as Presbyterians and then, influenced by radical Puritan doctrine and the translated works of continental mystics, progressed to sectarianism. Historians have spilt unnecessary ink discussing the relative influences of radical Puritanism and continental mysticism upon early Quakerism. The Quakers seem to have drawn on both traditions. Henry Clark, a Quaker friend of the Leveller John Lilburne, quoted from William Dell's *Testimony Against Divinity*. Richard Farnworth, one of the earliest converts to Quakerism, was influenced by the writings of John Saltmarsh. The library of Benjamin Furly contained works by Dell, Saltmarsh, John Everard, Giles Randall and William Erbery (all radical Puritan writers recommended by another leading Quaker, William Penn). Fox owned tracts by Dell and Thomas Collier. Other Quakers were influenced by John Webster, Peter Sterry, Walter Cradock, and Morgan Llwyd.[44] The library of Furly also contained pamphlets by the German mystic Jacob Boehme. Lodowick Muggleton doubtless exaggerated when he claimed that 'Jacob Behment's [i.e. Boehme's] Books were the chief Books that the Quakers bought', but Quakers did read Boehme (available in English translation in the 1640s and 1650s) and quoted him with approval. Rhys Johns, a Quaker schismatic from Nottingham, preached to groups of Behmenists as well as Quakers. A twentieth-century devotee of Boehme has described George Fox's *Journal* as 'full of Boehme's ideas and terminology', but it is difficult to be certain of influences as both authors drew upon the imagery of the Bible. Ironically, the London Morning Meeting of the Society of Friends was invoking the language of Boehme when it concluded, rather critically, that his ideas were a 'great mixture of light & darkness'.[45] Geoffrey Nuttall has traced other links with Familism.[46] And we have the suggestion that in the diocese of Ely Quakerism took hold in areas previously receptive to the Family of Love.[47] The interaction between radical Puritanism and continental mysticism can best be illustrated by the cases of William Erbery and Morgan Llwyd, both Puritans who were influenced by the ideas of Boehme. Interestingly, both men preached in Bristol in the early 1650s and were seen by a contemporary as preparing the way for Quakerism. Interestingly, Erbery's wife and daughter and members of Llwyd's Welsh congregation became Quakers.[48]

As we have seen, some of the early Quakers were what have been called Seekers, those who taught that people should 'sit still, in submission and silence, waiting for the Lord to come and reveal himself to them'. Bristol Quakerism began 'amongst a seeking people who kept one day in the week for fasting and praying, waiting for . . . [the] visitation of God and day of redemption'.[49] When Quakers entered a new area they seem to have carried lists of advanced separatists residing in that area, those most likely to be receptive to the Quaker message. When John Audland and his companions arrived in Bristol in 1654, they were directed to one Abraham Morris's house and told that they 'would find a people there who would discerne us, whether we were of God or no'.[50] Again and again sectaries were converted, sometimes whole meetings: Congregationalists, many Baptists, Seekers, some Ranters and Fifth Monarchists.[51]

When talking of the early 1650s 'conversion' is probably an inappropriate word to use. There is good evidence for Cambridgeshire that 'spiritual seeking and unrest was extremely widespread . . . and that the Quaker position was reached, or nearly reached, before the arrival of the Quakers'.[52] In Essex, this time several years before the Quakers arrived, the vicar of the parish of Earls Colne complained of the 'unreverent carriage' of several parishioners who had sat with their hats on throughout the singing of psalms, and of the opinions of one Robert Nichols of Colne Engaine who had spoken out for adult baptism yet who had claimed (like the Quakers) that he had not been baptized himself 'because baptizers give not the holy ghost'. By 1656 there were Quakers in Earls Colne; Robert Nichols had joined the sect; and Colne Engaine was being described by the same minister as 'the quakers nest'.[53]

Radical connections were not limited to the theological sphere. As we noted above, several northern Quakers had been involved in anti-tithe activity in their pre-Quaker days. The same was true of other parts of the country: Somerset, Kent, Essex, Suffolk, for example. Many Quakers had a history of active resistance to tithes. Unlike the Levellers, the Quakers responded to agrarian grievances; indeed during the Revolution they were among the most unrelenting opposers of tithes.[54]

Then there were the radical political links. Four former members of Barebone's Parliament became Quakers: Edward Plumstead (Suffolk), Alexander Jaffray and John Swinton (Scotland), and Dennis Hollister (Bristol).[55] In High Wycombe, Bristol, and Colchester there were conversions among radical aldermen and councillors, although the overall numbers were small.[56] More Quakers had been county committee men and sequestrators for Parliament, representatives of the new power elite of the 1640s: Robert Wastfield, James Pearce, Jasper Batt, and Christopher Pittard in Somerset; George Lamboll, Thomas Curtis, and Christopher Cheesman in Berkshire; Humphrey Lower in Cornwall; Francis Comberford in Staffordshire; John Fallowfield and Gervase Benson in Westmorland; Anthony Pearson in Durham; others in Wales.[57]

A few Quakers had been in the Navy; Daniel Baker and Anthony Mellidge had been officers. But it was the New Model Army that was a major source of Quaker recruitment. It has been claimed recently that the radical temper of the New Model has been much exaggerated both by conservative contemporaries such as Richard Baxter and Clement Walker and by later historians such as Christopher Hill. In absolute terms Mark Kishlansky is probably right: religious radicals did not dominate the Army.[58] But this is not to say that the Army was not an important nurturer of radical ideas, particularly if we look below the level of the senior officers and official chaplains to the lay preachers among the common soldiers and junior officers.[59]

The prehistory and history of Quakerism certainly reinforce this point. Early oral tradition recalls the future Quaker leader James Nayler, yeoman, quartermaster in Lambert's forces in Scotland, preaching after the battle of Dunbar (1650): 'I was struck with more terror before the preaching of James Nayler than I was before the battle of Dunbar. . . . The people there, in the clear and powerful opening of their states, cried out against themselves, imploring mercy, a thorough change and the whole work of salvation to be effected in them.'[60] Nayler, Richard Hubberthorne, Edward Billing, John Crook, Gervase Benson, Edward Cook, Amos Stoddart, William Morris, Thomas Curtis, George Bishop, Edward Pyott, Francis Gawler, Joseph Fuce, all Quakers whom we shall encounter in this volume, were officers in the New Model. George Fox the younger, William Dewsbury, Benjamin Nicholson, William Edmundson, John Whitehead, John and Thomas Stubbs, and William Ames served in the ranks. Richard Vann refers to ninety-five Quakers who had served in the Parliamentary forces; but there were many more.[61] When 'we first engaged in the Wars', some Quaker veterans wrote in 1657, 'Liberty of Conscience, and the true Freedom of the Nations from all their oppressions, was the Mark at which we aimed'.[62] By becoming Quakers they felt that they were continuing the struggle. When General George Monck purged some forty Quaker soldiers from his forces in Scotland in 1657, none of those dismissed had been in the Army for less than seven years, and the majority had service records of fourteen years which means that they had joined up at the beginning of the civil war.[63]

We shall see later that influential military support was an important factor when it comes to explaining the establishment of the early Quaker movement. Quakers met in the home of Robert Overton, the Fifth Monarchist governor of Hull.[64] Robert Lilburne, Governor of York, was also sympathetic; 'we have great friendshipe, and love from ye governer of the Towne', Thomas Aldam reported in 1652, 'and many of ye souldiers are very sollid'.[65] Lilburne's regiment, one of the most mutinous regiments at the time of the Leveller agitation in the 1640s, was receptive to the Quaker message. Two troop commanders (William Bradford and George Watkinson) turned Quaker, and Edward Hickhorngill, Lilburne's apostate Baptist chaplain, thought the Quakers midway between his own sect and a 'higher dispensation'.[66] In Bristol too, as the Corporation's Presbyterian chaplain complained, the sect was 'upheld, countenanced, maintained, and propagated . . . by the strength and power of these Souldiers'. The Governor, Colonel Adrian Scrope, was not unsympathetic and several of his men became Quakers.[67] The officer in charge of the garrison at Holy Island (Northumberland), Henry Phillips, became a Quaker and permitted his soldiers to hold meetings.[68] Lawrence Knott, commander of Sandgate Castle and yet another convert, performed a similar service in Kent.[69]

Contemporaries claimed that Levellers and Diggers had become Quakers. 'Wast thou not at Burford among the Levellers?', a JP asked Nayler in 1653.[70] 'Several Levellers setled into Quakers', wrote John Ward, vicar of Stratford-upon-Avon;

and he claimed that the 'draught and bodie' of Quakerism was 'to bee found in ye works of Gerard Winstanley', the Digger leader.[71] Ward's suggestions are at least plausible. Leveller and True Leveller or Digger ideas do recur in Quaker literature. Winstanley and the Leveller leader John Lilburne became Quakers, as did Lilburne's friend Henry Clark and George Bishop.[72] The Quaker Christopher Cheesman, a friend of the Leveller activist William Bray, was also a former Leveller. In 1649 he denied the accusation that he had been 'one of the chief in the late mutiny of the Army', but was outspoken in his defence of Bray and condemnation of the military elite and Oliver Cromwell ('one of the Achans that trouble the Peace of Israel') whom he saw as the betrayers of the Revolution. Cheesman appealed to the people: 'And, shall you true-hearted people of England, be wise, and do justice upon all the Achans, send them after the late King, and then stick close to the Agreement put forth by our friends in the Tower.'[73] We know that the Quakers were successful with the regiment of Robert Lilburne, a force notorious for its rebelliousness at the time of Leveller agitation in the Army. We know that several Digger parishes later contained Quakers.[74] Yet there is no evidence of any substantial continuity between Levellers and Diggers and Quakers.

So occasionally Quakerism appealed to men of influence, those to whom power had shifted in the 1640s, radical ex-MPs, committee men, councillors, military officers. But the majority of early Friends were people from outside the governing circle, whether old or new; men and women of radical political and religious persuasion, uninfluential figures already engaged in a spiritual quest and, sometimes, in more material struggle.

IV

We are now quite well informed about the social origins of the Quakers of the 1650s and 1660s, for there is a considerable literature on the subject.[75] Although there was, as we shall see, regional variation in the movement's social composition, it seems that it mainly drew its membership from what were known as the 'middling sort of people': wholesale and retail traders, artisans, yeomen, husbandmen. Those, with the exceptions of Quaker women and husbandmen, from the more literate – or rather less illiterate – sections of the population.[76] Few belonged to the gentry elite, few to the *labouring* poor. Hearth-tax returns, which permit a socio-economic profile of the early Quakers in comparison with the general population, suggest likewise that though there were substantial numbers of the poorer sort in the movement, most belonged to the relatively comfortable middle section of the community and were slightly wealthier than the population at large. So the picture we have is somewhat more complex than that provided by Alan Cole in 1957 when he claimed that the sect was drawn mainly from the urban and rural petty bourgeoisie, or indeed that suggested by Richard Vann's more recent and rigorous analysis which stressed the prominence of the 'upper bourgeoisie', the yeomen and the wholesale traders.[77]

A glance at Tables 1 and 2 will reveal that a significant number of the early Quakers were yeomen; the county percentages range from 20.4 per cent of Norfolk Quakers for whom occupations are known to 28.9 per cent for Essex. In a narrow legal sense the term yeoman meant a freeholder of land worth over 40s. per annum, but in common usage it was used 'to describe any well-to-do farmer beneath the rank of gentleman, even though he was not a freeholder'.[78] In other words, the category included substantial copyholders or leaseholders. The Quaker yeomen ranged from Andrew Smith of Stebbing (Essex) who owed £9 in tithes for his 80-acre arable holding, who was rated at four hearths in the 1662 hearth-tax returns, and who left bequests of some £200 in 1675, to Christopher Pittard, the Trent (Somerset) yeoman, whose bequests in 1679 amount to over £1,000, and who owned estates in some five Somerset parishes.[79] Many were men of wealth, but the evidence from Cheshire and Somerset suggests that, in these counties at least, Quaker yeomen tended to be leaseholders and copyholders, able to vote yet excluded from the governing structure of the local community which required substantial *freehold* status.[80] (Whether this ambivalent status had anything to do with their attraction to Quakerism, however, must remain conjectural.)

There were also a substantial number of Quaker wholesale traders and large producers, often, as with the yeomen, men of some means: merchants, clothiers, millers, maltsters and so on. On a grander scale, they were men like Robert Beard, a tanner from Theydon Garnon in Essex, who employed at least five servants, and who, when he died, left various lands and tenements, bequests of some £400, and an annuity of £30; or

Table 1 Occupational distribution of Quakers c. 1654–1664 (in percentages of those with known occupations)*

Occupation or Status	Cheshire	Essex	Colchester	Somerset
Gentry	3.2	2.5	13.3	–
Professional	1.3	–	3.3	–
Agricultural	59.7	55.4	–	62.1
Yeomen	21.4	28.9	–	24.3
Farmers	22.1	17.4	–	16.9
Husbandmen	16.2	9.1	–	20.9
Wholesale Traders and Large Producers (e.g. Clothiers)	3.2	15.7	43.3	13.0
Retail Traders	14.9	11.6	20.0	9.6
Artisans	13.0	11.6	20.0	12.4
Labourers and Servants	4.5	3.3	–	2.8

Table 2 Occupational distribution of Quakers c. 1654–1664 (in percentages of those with known occupations)

Occupation or Status	Cheshire	Essex	Colchester	Somerset	Buckinghamshire	Norfolk	Norwich
Gentry	3.2	2.5	13.3	–	7.3	7.4	6.3
Professional	1.3	–	3.3	–	3.6	1.9	–
Agricultural (inc. Gentry)	63.0	57.9	–	62.1	45.5	35.2	–
Yeomen	21.4	28.9	–	24.3	27.3	20.4	–
Farmers	22.1	17.4	–	16.9	5.5	–	–
Husbandmen	16.2	9.1	–	20.9	1.8	5.6	–
Labourers/Servants	–	–	–	–	7.3	5.6	–
Wholesale Traders	3.2	9.1	20.0	6.2	25.5	18.5	12.5
Retail Traders	14.9	11.6	20.0	9.6	16.4	11.1	18.8
(Textile production): Weavers, Woolcombers, and Clothiers	5.2	9.1	40.0	9.6	–	16.7	43.8
Artisans	7.8	9.1	3.3	9.6		16.7	18.8
Servants and Labourers	4.5	3.3	–	2.8	9.1		

*See note on page 31 for sources.

No. of Hearths	County (Select Parishes)		Quakers (Same Select Parishes)		Quakers (Whole County)	
	No. of Houses	%	No. of Houses	%	No. of Houses	%
CHESHIRE	(1,202)		(71)		(142)	
(6+)	(17)	(1.4)	(–)	(–)	(1)	(0.7)
3+ (large houses – prosperous)	90	7.5	10	14.1	19	13.4
2 (modest houses – comfortable)	151	12.6	21	29.6	33	23.2
1 (?)	567	47.2	39	54.9	80	56.3
exempt (small houses, cottages – poor)	394	32.8	1	1.4	10	7.0
	mean no. of hearths 1.4				mean no. of hearths 1.6	
ESSEX	(1,275)		(67)		(170)	
(8+)	(21)	(1.6)	(–)	(–)	(7)	(4.1)
4+ (large houses – prosperous)	243	19.1	25	37.3	66	38.8
2-3 (modest houses – comfortable)	306	24.0	29	43.3	65	38.2
exempt–1 (small houses, cottages – poor)	726	56.9	13	19.4	39 (13 exempt)	22.9
	mean no. of hearths 2.3				mean no. of hearths 3.3	
SOMERSET	(1,594)		(64)		(141)	
(8+)	(22)	(1.4)	(–)	(–)	(–)	(–)
4+ (large houses – prosperous)	149	9.3	11	17.2	22	15.6
2-3 (modest houses – comfortable)	485	30.4	35	54.7	71	50.4
exempt–1 (small houses, cottages – poor)	960	60.2	18	28.1	48 (26 exempt)	34.0
	mean no. of hearths 2.0				mean no. of hearths 2.3	

William Talcott, a Colchester stapler, who owned a great deal of freehold and copyhold land, several houses, and over 300 acres of woodland in various parts of Essex, and who bequeathed several £20 annuities and over £1,000 in 1698.[81] Men such as these Quaker merchants and yeomen and the occasional convert from the gentry ('greate ones in the outward') were important for nurturing the movement once it had struck its often shallow roots in a particular region. William Gandy of Over Whitley in Great Budworth, Cheshire, Jasper Batt of Street in Somerset, the Furlys of Colchester, became what one Quaker described as 'good harbers for Frends'.[82] And as Vann has suggested, it was probably the wholesalers in the movement, mobile and articulate, travelling from market to market and picking up new ideas, who were responsible for much of the spread of the Quaker message.[83]

But the material that we now have (summarized in Tables 1-3), does not support Vann's suggestion that the above groups *predominated* in early Quakerism. The figures for Somerset, Cheshire, and Essex – 20.9 per cent, 16.2 per cent, and 9.1 per cent – suggest rather more husbandmen in the movement than Vann was prepared to allow; and a recent Lancashire survey by Alan Anderson has found that Quaker husbandmen (46.1 per cent) *outnumbered* Quaker yeomen (36.9 per cent).[84] So these smaller landholders, farmers below yeomen in rank, were by no means a negligible component of the early movement. The same is true of artisans and retailers – blacksmiths, shoemakers, tailors, butchers, weavers, carpenters – who seem to have been quite numerous (Cheshire 27.9 per cent, Essex 23.2 per cent, Colchester 40 per cent, Somerset 22 per cent). Vann's claim that a Quaker was more likely to be a wholesaler or a large producer than an artisan or retailer may be true of Colchester, Norwich, Buckinghamshire, and Norfolk: it was not true of Cheshire, Essex, or Somerset. The early Quaker movement was not as comfortably bourgeois as Vann would have it.

And it now seems that there were rather fewer Quaker gentlemen than Vann had projected with his figures of 6.3 per cent, 7.3 per cent, and 7.4 per cent for Norwich, Buckinghamshire, and Norfolk. Apart from Colchester, which is in any case something of an aberration,[85] the other percentages which we have are considerably lower than Vann's: 0 for Somerset, 2 for Warwickshire, 2.5 for Essex, 3.2 for Cheshire, 3.9 for Lancashire.[86] And four of the five Cheshire 'gentlemen' were yeomen who had been awarded gentry status, presumably because of their families' service in the grand jury. [87]

All the recent surveys are agreed, however, that the number of Quaker servants and labourers was minimal. Although the hearth-tax returns, [88] a rough standard-of-living index (see Table 3), indicate that there was a solid core of the poorer sort to be found in Somerset and Essex Quakerism, and presumably in Cheshire too, the movement was drawn mainly from the middling sort; it was wealthier than the general population. The Quakers of the 1650s and early 1660s were not 'the dregs of the common people', as contemporaries alleged, 'the Refuse of the World, Persons of the meanest Quality and lowest Parts and Education'. [89]

Equally clearly, large percentages of the early Quakers were involved in agriculture: 86.9 in Lancashire, 63 in Cheshire, 62.1 in Somerset, 57.9 in Essex, 46 in Warwickshire, 45.5 in Buckinghamshire, 35.2 in Norfolk. [90] Many more lived in rural areas, though they were engaged in non-agricultural village trades. Quakerism was predominantly a rural movement.

There was great regional variation in the social structure of early Quakerism. Buckinghamshire Quakerism, for instance, with its high percentages of gentry, wholesale traders, and yeomen, contrasts with that of Cheshire and Somerset where there were fewer gentlemen and wholesalers, and rather more husbandmen. Or if we use the hearth-tax returns as a crude guide to wealth, we find that Warwickshire Quakers [91] were poorer, and Essex Quakers wealthier, than their co-religionists elsewhere. If the Norwich and Colchester figures are any indication, we can probably assume that where the local economy was dominated by the textile industry, large numbers of Quakers were employed in trades connected with these manufactures. [92]

Yet despite this variation, the overall social complexion of the Quaker movement of the 1650s and 1660s is quite clear. In their study of the Essex parish of Terling, Keith Wrightson and David Levine found that the village Quakers consisted of two yeomen, two husbandmen, an innkeeper, a millwright, and a grocer. [93] Here, at micro-level, is what I have suggested is to be found at macro-level. Quakerism was essentially an affair of the middling sort. It was more plebeian than Vann's pioneering work suggested. It was also, above all, rural.

One final point has to be made when discussing the social

composition of the early movement: women joined the Quakers in large numbers. By 1662 they comprised 40-50 per cent of Norwich, Norfolk, and Buckinghamshire Quakers, and Vann's figures must be an underestimation.[94] The sect did not offer women equality, but certainly more independence than that offered by society. The Quaker husband was still 'the head of the Wife, even as Christ is the head of the Church'.[95] But the light within did lead to a kind of spiritual equality: 'Christ in the Male, and in the Female is one'. George Fox believed that the subjection of women was the result of the Fall of Man: 'in the restoration by Christ . . . they are helps meet, Man and Woman, as they were before'.[96]

Quaker women preached, proselytized, wrote and printed tracts, participated in church government (though in separate meetings and mainly in the area of welfare),[97] and assumed a militant role in the sect's various campaigns. Mary Dyer was executed as a Quaker in New England in 1660 for her persistent challenging of the harsh laws of Boston. The Yorkshire Quaker Ann Blaykling tramped the length and breadth of England, apparently forgetting that she was of the 'weaker sex'. We can trace her movements by her encounters with the authorities: in York in 1654 (in trouble for interrupting a minister), in Cambridge later the same year (in trouble for vagrancy), in London in 1655 (when she spoke to the Protector), in Norfolk in 1655 (vagrancy), in Cornwall and Suffolk in 1656 (again in trouble), and in prison in Suffolk in 1659.[98] Of 360 Quakers in trouble for disrupting ministers during the period 1654 to 1659, 34 per cent were women; of the fifty-nine Quaker 'ministers' who arrived in America during the period 1656 to 1663, 45 per cent were women.[99] Gone was the old precept: 'Let your women learn in silence, with all subjection'.[100]

v

It is extremely difficult to determine the actual number of Quakers at the end of their first decade, and any conclusions must be tentative. The Quaker Samuel Fisher was hopelessly out of touch (unless he was referring to adult males only) when he wrote in 1660 that there were seven thousand of the 'people of Christ' in England. Opponents put their strength higher: 'above thirty thousand', according to John Gaskin; 150,000 according to Thomas Underhill, though he appears to have included other sectaries (he used the word 'Quaker' rather loosely).[101]

Subsequent estimations have more or less agreed with the more conservative figures provided by contemporaries: between thirty and forty thousand at the Restoration, according to W. C. Braithwaite; about forty thousand by the end of the century, according to M. R. Watts.[102] My own calculations suggest numbers slightly higher: certainly between thirty-five and forty thousand by the early 1660s; possibly sixty thousand.[103] The Quakers were the most successful of the Revolution sects; but they still comprised less than 1 per cent of the total population of England.

The geography of early Quakerism has yet to be written. Our present knowledge of the distribution of the movement in its early years is based mainly on the work of Hugh Barbour, who has located three main areas of Quaker strength during the 1650s: the North, 'the crucial region of early Quakerism' (Yorkshire, northern Lancashire, Westmorland, and Cumberland); London, the second Quaker stronghold; and a section of the West of England (Bristol, Somerset, and Gloucestershire), 'the third great region . . . after London and the North Country'.[104] The trouble with Barbour's impressions is that they are based almost entirely on the geographical origins of Quaker 'ministers' and pamphlet and letter writers, so consequently ignore many of the Quaker rank and file. But his observations are a useful starting point. Barbour's general thesis is that Quakerism moved either into 'untouched territory' as 'an "awakening" among the unchurched', or into areas where Puritan influence was fragmentary or weak – that is, satellite villages near Puritan urban strongholds. He stresses that the heartlands of Puritanism were 'cold' to Quakerism: Norfolk, Suffolk, Essex, Cambridgeshire, and most of the south-east.[105]

We are not yet in a position to rank *all* English counties according to their adherence to Quakerism as Michael Watts has for the early eighteenth century;[106] but it is at least possible – using various county studies, a Quaker women's anti-tithe petition of 1659, and the lists of the numbers of Quakers arrested in early 1661 – to supplement, modify, and (in some instances) challenge the findings of Barbour.[107] My calculations tend to reinforce his claims for the geographical importance of Bristol and London: Bristol with its 1,000 Quakers, or 5.6 per cent of the city's population; London with 8,000–10,000 Quakers, or

Map 1 Major Areas of Quakerism 1654–64

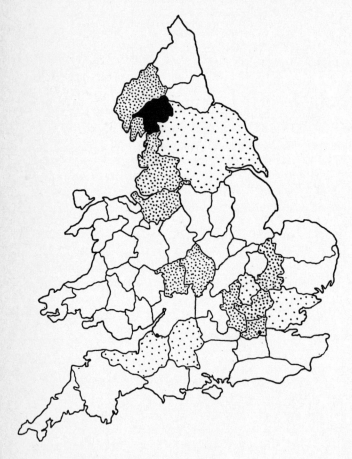

Percentages of Total Population

 0·8 – 1·0
1·0 – 2·0
over 3·0

something like 1.5 per cent of the total city population. (In the nation at large, Quakers comprised 0.8 per cent of the population.) The counties of the North, Barbour's other great area of Quakerism, are above the national Quaker average, but sometimes the difference is marginal: 1,000 Quakers in Westmorland (3.3 per cent of the total population); over 800 Quakers in Cumberland (1.3 per cent of the total population); 1,300 Quakers in Cheshire (1.2 per cent of the total population); 2,000 Quakers in Lancashire (1.0 per cent of the total population); 4,300 Quakers in Yorkshire (0.9 per cent of the total population). If we talk in terms of numbers of Quakers – almost 10,000 in five counties – then the importance of the North seems hard to dispute. But if one thinks more in terms of *percentages of the total population*, the old orthodoxy about the relative success of Quakerism in the North will have to be revised.[108] This becomes clear if the figures above are compared with the strengths of Quaker populations in areas for the most part neglected by Barbour: Warwickshire 1.6 per cent, Worcestershire 1.6 per cent, Hertfordshire 1.5 per cent, Buckinghamshire 1.0 per cent, Bedfordshire 0.9 per cent, Wiltshire 0.8 per cent, Somerset 0.8 per cent. Nor is there much evidence of under-representation of Quakerism in the supposedly 'cold' areas of the east. In Cambridgeshire probably 1.6 per cent of the population was Quaker; and the figure for Essex, 0.8 per cent, is exactly the same as the national average.[109]

The picture that emerges, then, is rather more complicated than Barbour's tripartite division. There were in fact four main areas of Quaker strength in the 1650s and early 1660s: (1) the North, including Cheshire (not on Barbour's list of the northern Quaker heartlands); (2) London *and* a group of counties directly north and east (Buckinghamshire, Hertfordshire, Bedfordshire, Cambridgeshire, and Essex); (3) Bristol, Somerset, and Wiltshire (though not Gloucestershire); (4) the two counties Warwickshire and Worcestershire. (See Map 1.)[110]

But the crucial point about the early Quaker movement is its widespread penetration of the counties. As I said at the beginning of this chapter, all counties were affected. The nature of this Quaker penetration cannot yet be demonstrated in detail on a national scale, but it is possible to provide examples at the local level. Maps 2-4 plot the distribution of Quakers in the counties of Cheshire, Essex, and Somerset at the end of the ten-year period

Maps 2–4 Distribution of Quakers 1654–64

(Shaded areas represent parishes with *at least one* Quaker family)

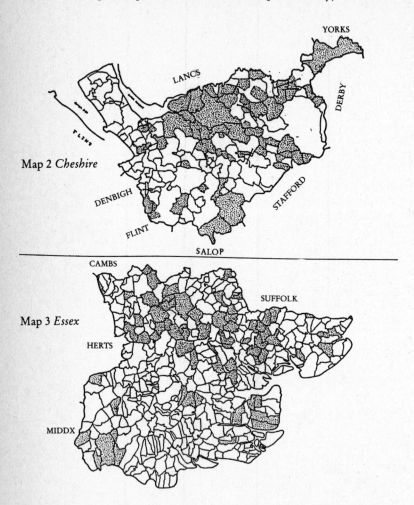

Map 2 *Cheshire*

Map 3 *Essex*

1654-1664.[111] The counties chosen represent a good regional cross-section – the North, East Anglia, and the West. None have exactly been celebrated for the strength of their attachment to Quakerism. So the Quaker impact (plotted on maps of these three counties) is all the more impressive. Quakerism was remarkable not for its total membership, but for the sheer scope of its impact.

Map 4 *Somerset*

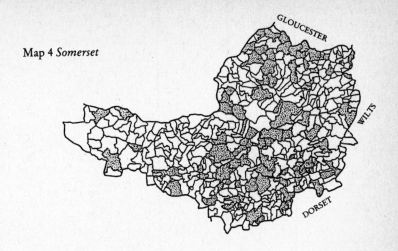

Note on Tables 1-3 (pages 22-3): The information on Cheshire, Essex, Colchester and Somerset is based on my own work, summarized in *Journal of Interdisciplinary History*, xi (1980). The figures for Buckinghamshire, Norfolk and Norwich come from Vann, *Social Development*, 59-60.

CHAPTER 2
Early Quakerism

I

Quakerism was very much a creature of its age, part of the radicalism and enthusiasm of the revolutionary years. It was successful – and its success during the early years was phenomenal – because it responded to the needs of that time. Like all millenarian movements (I use the term in its broadest sense), Quakerism was a response to upheaval, significantly a product of the second and not the first decade of the Revolution. The rising expectations which civil war had unleashed were frustrated, halted midway, and Quakerism was one of the forms which disillusionment took. But converts to the Quaker message were not simply seeking consolation in religion after their political defeat.[1] Nor did Quakerism save the nation from the 'spectre of radicalism', as was suggested some time ago in an argument reminiscent of earlier claims for eighteenth- and nineteenth-century Methodism.[2] What A. L. Morton has described as the loss of 'aggressive radicalism' may have been true of the majority of Quakers *after* 1660: it was certainly not true of them before that date.[3] Indeed, one might say that after the defeat of the Levellers and the Diggers and the downfall of the Rump and Barebone's Parliaments, the Quakers were the only group capable of representing the aspirations of earlier years. Spiritual regeneration would ensure the political, social, and religious millennium; this time there would be no compromise or duplicity. The sect became the conscience of the radical, republican cause, the 'Good Old Cause'. 'Wilstandley [i.e. Gerrard Winstanley] sayes he beleeves we are sent to perfect that worke which fell in their handes hee hath bene with us', the Quaker Edward Burrough reported in 1654 after his meeting in London with the Digger leader.[4] In short, Quakerism was 'a movement of protest against the suppression of the "good old cause"'.[5]

II

The Quakers of the Interregnum were not preoccupied with theology; it was only later, in the 1670s, that they set out their religious doctrine in any systematic form. Before that, in the words of Christopher Hill, they usually defined their beliefs defensively, 'by negatives'.[6]

Quakers rejected predestinarian doctrine and proclaimed the possibility of salvation for all: 'God woulde have all men to bee saved Marke all men.' They argued that Calvin's theory of predestination – the doctrine that 'God, by His eternal goodwill, . . . destined those whom He pleased to salvation, rejecting the rest' – would have God 'the most Cruel of all Beings'. They urged men and women to turn to the light, Christ, spirit within (they used the terms interchangeably). We 'call All men to look to the Light within their own consciences', wrote the Quaker Samuel Fisher; 'by the leadings of that Light, if they will, they may come to God, and work out their Salvation'.[7] Of course, not everyone would be saved: 'we talk of an universal Redemption by Christ's coming intentionally to save All men, though (through their own default) All are not, but few only actually saved'. Quakers could still talk in terms of the 'generation of Cain' and the seed of 'righteous Abel'.[8] But the important point is that the accent was on human effort. Quakerism provided an answer to the simple question, 'How can I be saved?'

There was a strong sense of unity with God. Not all Quakers were as outspoken as Thomas Holme who declared that he was 'above St Peter & equall with god', but most would have agreed with George Fox when he said that 'He that sanctifieth, and they that are sanctified, are of one, and the Saints are all one in the Father and the Son'.[9] God spoke directly to his people and through his people. 'I would faine have omited words in them Both', William Gibson said of some papers he had written, 'but I durst not For ye power of ye Lord wch Rose in mee was triable agt them.' Quaker schismatics were said to have forsaken 'the devine sap & vertue of Crist Jeesus'.[10] Indeed, as prophets of the new age, those 'in the power and spirit of God' were expected to have visions and revelations. God manifested his power through 'his servants'. Fox had many dreams and revelations, most of which were purged from the first edition of his *Journal*. When James Milner, a Quaker tailor from Furness in Lancashire, declared in 1652 that Wednesday the first of December would be the Day of Judgement and that the New Creation would begin the day after, he was being impolitically precise. But Fox and several others did at various stages claim that they had predicted Pride's Purge, the death of Cromwell, the Restoration, the Dutch War, and the Plague and the Fire of London.[11]

The notion of the light within – an extension of the Puritan emphasis on the Holy Spirit – is central to Quaker religious ideology.[12] They were spiritual millenarians. 'The coming of Christ in the flesh . . . was one coming . . . and his appearance in Spirit to save his people from sin; is another coming', wrote George Whitehead in 1660. Christ had come in Quakers and would come in others; social and political change would accompany this inward millennium.[13]

Like other radicals, the Quakers thought that the spirit was above the Scriptures. It was the uneducated man's and woman's way of rejecting the hegemony of a learned elite. The emphasis varied. When Baptists in the Huntingdonshire–Cambridgeshire area turned Quaker they argued that the 'light in their consciences was the rule they desire to walk by', not the Scriptures. The 'conscience was above the scriptures; and the scriptures ought to be tried by it, and not that by the scriptures'.[14] Barbara Siddall said that the Bible was 'not the word of God but onely a dead letter'; Katherine Crook, 'Shee had Knowne ye Lord if Shee had never seene nor read ye Scriptures'.[15] Other Quakers would have been shocked by such talk, but again few would have argued with Fox's claim that it was 'not the letter, nor the writing of the Scripture, but the ingrafted Word is able to save your soules'.[16] Indeed, Samuel Fisher was to subject the Bible to close critical analysis. The effect, according to Christopher Hill, was to 'demote the Bible from its central position in the protestant scheme of things, to make it a book like any other'.[17]

The sect rejected conventional ideas about the Trinity: the doctrine of three distinguishable identities. 'God and the Spirit hath no Person, nor cannot truly be distinguished into Persons'.[18] Francis Howgil, one of the better-known Quakers, disregarded notions of 'God at a distance'.[19] The Quakers, wrote Cotton Mather, 'scoffed at our imagined God beyond the stars'.[20] As far as Christ was concerned, T. L. Underwood has explained, 'the outward physical work of Christ in the past was of little consequence without an inward, spiritual experience of Christ by men in the present'.[21] The implication was that the historic role of Christ was of little more import than the role of any leading Quaker.

Quaker eschatology was equally unorthodox. The tendency was to internalize, with the emphasis once again upon the present. They did not actually deny that there would be a Final Judgement and Resurrection, but the stress was on the resurrection and judgement within each Quaker. 'The great judgment is already begun (this we know, who have tasted of it).'[22] There was a tendency to talk of Heaven and Hell as internal states. Heaven was in the hearts of God's people: Hell was to be found in the conscience of every malefactor.[23] The Baptist Matthew Caffyn reported that when he had asked a Quaker 'where that Heaven was that Christ ascended up into', the Quaker had replied, 'clapping his hands upon his breast', 'WITHIN MEE, WITHIN MEE'. Nathaniel Smith claimed that he was attracted to Quakerism because of its belief that 'the Kingdom of Heaven was in Man'.[24]

III

People are not always aware that the early Quakers were essentially an ecstatic movement, that like the Shakers their name derives from their behaviour – that is, trembling and shaking. Quaking was an outward manifestation of the inward workings of the power of God. In London in 1654 when Quakers first visited the city, women cried while Richard Hubberthorne preached and Edward Burrough trembled; 'almost all ye Roome was Shaken', Richard Farnworth reported of another early meeting, this time in Yorkshire.[25]

Quaker perfectionism (the doctrine that believers could become free from sin), their belief in the potential powers of the light within, could lead to bizarre behaviour, particularly when the individual concerned was steeped in biblical imagery and plagued by Puritan preoccupations with the Devil. John Gilpin crawled up a street in Kendal, 'thinking that I bore a Crosse upon my neck'. The spirit within 'moved' the one-time Quaker John Toldervy to put his hand in a pan of boiling water, to burn his leg by the fire, and to thrust a needle into his thumbs (to the bone).[26] Some looked, according to anti-Quaker writers, for signs from Heaven in the form of stones or flies, or they thought that the Devil was being cast out, metamorphosed into a 'Knat or a Flie'.[27]

Extravagant behaviour and perfectionist claims became the

badge of divine approbation, symbolically setting the Quakers apart from the ungodly. Thus George Emmot, a gentleman from Durham, tore off his fine clothes and ribbons and dressed himself in plain garb and a hat with a piece of string in place of a hatband. 'In this same garb I thought my selfe not worldly, but all spiritual'; he was the new man, the very archetype of the sectarian who severs himself from society.[28] Several Quakers went 'naked as a sign'; as testimony to the spiritual nakedness of the world, as a forewarning that all pride would be cast aside at the Last Judgement, and as a symbol of their regenerate nature (Adam and Eve had gone naked before the Fall).[29] Such 'signs' were highly symbolic and clearly intended to shock. Sarah Goldsmith walked through Bristol market in 1655 with her 'haire about her eares', bare legged, and clad only in a 'long hairy coat'.[30] Richard Sale, a Quaker tailor from Hoole (near Chester), stood clothed in sackcloth with flowers in one hand and weeds in the other, and ashes sprinkled in his hair.[31] Solomon Eccles, a former music teacher from London who had burned his instruments and some books when he turned Quaker, walked through Smithfield naked, with a pan of burning coals upon his head.[32] Quaker shopkeepers in Malton burned silks and ribbons as a testimony against extravagance; there was no justification for such frills while people remained poor and unclothed.[33]

Perfectionism led several married Quakers in New England into a sexual abstinence which lasted for up to four years – 'some weare neare besids them selves about it'.[34] And Fox, it is often said, claimed to have progressed beyond such things: 'I Judged such things as below mee'.[35] Such tests of endurance were unusual and, Fox excepted, the individuals concerned were sometimes on the fringes of the movement. Yet better-known Quakers found it necessary to demonstrate divine approval in other ways. Christ had fasted: so could the Quakers. James Nayler, Fox, and many others fasted for seven, twelve, and even twenty days. Hubberthorne was so weak after a fast 'people thought hee was dead'. James Parnell did die (in Colchester gaol) after taking nothing but water for ten days.[36]

Some claimed the ability to heal and work miracles. As Farnworth wrote, God manifested his power in 'his servants' so that they could 'lay hands on the sick, and recover them, as the Apostles did'.[37] There are traces too of the Hermetic tradition, a belief that man has fallen out with the creation but that in a state of perfection (of restoration) unity can once more be achieved and nature's secrets revealed.[38] A few Quaker women claimed that they had experienced painless childbirth.[39] Fox kept a record of his cures, some 150 in all: smallpox, scrofula (the King's Evil), dumbness, ague, toothache, the stone, convulsions, scabs, headache, ulcers, gout, blindness, paralysis, a broken neck. Few claimed the successes of Fox. Francis Howgil failed in his attempt to cure a lame boy: 'the boy stode up but . . . he fayled and sat downe agayne'.[40] One or two were even more ambitious and attempted to raise the dead. A Worcester Quaker dug up the corpse of a Quaker apprentice and 'commanded him in the name of the living God, to arise and walk'. It was said that Quakers travelled to Colchester to see the resurrection of their co-religionist James Parnell after his death in prison in 1656.[41]

IV

The success of Quakerism, Christopher Hill has reminded us, witnessed to the continued existence of the radicalism of the 1640s.[42] Perhaps it was this that Winstanley had in mind in 1654 when he told Burrough that the Quakers were carrying on the work of the Diggers.[43]

Certainly they inherited the anticlericalism of the Revolution radicals. According to the Quakers, the whole ecclesiastical edifice was rotten. The clergy were more concerned with their bellies than with their parishioners' souls. When a priest dies, Fox wrote, his colleagues scramble for his benefice; 'they are like a company of crowes when a rotten sheepe is deade they all gather togeather to plucke out his puddinges'.[44] The insides of churches, like the fields, were enclosed: 'lined Stalls for the rich, with a lock and key to keep the poor out'.[45] Through the system of tithes, priests were maintained in 'idleness' by the 'labours of poor people'. The church owed its wealth to the labour of others; 'From whence I pray were these [riches] squeezed', Thomas Ellwood asked, 'was it not from the people?'[46] The clergy had kept the people in ignorance; indeed 'the People have been so foolish to give their money to be made blind, and to be led into the ditch'.

> Thou presses People to that which thou hast as much need as they to practise, Obedience and Patience, which thou calls the *shooes of the Gospel*. . . . Thou bids them be

content with such things as they have, though they have
but from hand to mouth; with food and rayment, though
they have no more. The poor it seems must be preached
unto patience and contentednesse without dainties and
Ornaments; but the Priests and the proud Ones, who live
in pomp and plenty, may purchase Lands and possessions
without check.[47]

Not only spiritual blindness was involved, for the priests were
agents of political reaction and had, suggested Joseph Fuce,
persuaded many a deluded individual to vote for an 'unfit'
parliamentary candidate.[48]

The Quakers called quite simply for the disestablishment of the
state church. God was no longer the preserve of the 'learned men
brought up at Universities'; he had 'chosen the foolish things, and
weak things, and base things, and despised things, to do his
works by'. 'Silly men and women', those whom 'the Scribes
called illiterate', wrote Priscilla Cotton and Mary Cole (Quaker
wives of a Plymouth merchant and a shopkeeper), 'know more of
the Messiah, then all the learned Priests and Rabbies'.[49] Men and
women should hire their own ministers or else ministers should
labour to support themselves. The Quakers wanted a movement
away from the university-bred, privileged clergy towards a
ministry of simple men and women 'who spoke plaine words, and
reached to the consciences of men of the meanest capacity'.[50]
They pressed too for religious toleration – a 'Naturall Right' –
and quoted Oliver Cromwell to good effect: 'had it not been for
the hopes of Liberty of Conscience, all the money in the Nation
would not have tempted men to fight'.[51] Hence – apart from
straightforward economic considerations – the importance of the
Quakers' campaign against tithes. England had been cleared of
kings and bishops; it was now time for their progeny, the
priesthood, to be 'taken away, disanulled and abolished'.[52] If the
priests lost their compulsory maintenance, wrote Burrough, they
would have to 'either beg, or work, or a worse thing for a
livelihood, or else perish'.[53] The Quakers organized petitions
against tithes. They organized support for parliamentary
candidates who were likely to be sympathetic to their cause: we
have evidence of this for 1656 and 1659: the regicide John
Bradshaw in Cheshire, John Lambert, possibly Robert Lilburne,
and their own aspirant William Bradford in Yorkshire.[54] And

they refused themselves to pay tithes, inciting others to follow them and in many cases actually leading opposition at the parish level. In short, the Quakers formed the vanguard of popular agitation against tithes.[55]

The Quakers did not limit themselves to criticism of the church and ministry. Some spoke out bravely against the nobility and gentry, claiming that they either owed their position to the Norman Conquest when their ancestors 'killed an English man, and took his possession', or had founded their families on 'fraud, deceit, and oppression'.

> Woe unto you that are called Lords, Ladies, Knights, Gentlemen, and Gentlewomen, in respect to your persons, who are exalted in the earth . . . who are called of men Master, and Sir . . . because of your much earth, which by fraud, deceit, and oppression you have gotten together, you are exalted above your fellow-creatures, and grind the faces of the poore, and they are as slaves under you, and must labour and toyle under you, and you must live at ease. . . .[56]

The 'Clargey & ye gentry, hath ye lande betwixt them', wrote Elizabeth Hooton. Edward Billing approved of the sentiments of those who had said that it 'would never be a good World so long as there was a Lord in England'; 'for the whole rabble of Duke, Marquesse, Lord, Knight Gentleman by patents; I find no room . . . in Scripture'.[57]

The law, the 'badge of the conquerour' according to Billing, also kept 'the poore people in bondage'. For the poor 'the remedy [was] frequently worse then the desease' when it came to using the law. Like property, protection was the prerogative of a few – 'the rich bears with the rich, and the poor have been trodden underfoot'.[58] Instead of 'covering the naked, and feeding the hungry, you set out Laws to punish them', Benjamin Nicholson complained in a pamphlet aimed at the magistrates of England.[59]

We can get some idea of the sort of society the Quakers would have envisaged. There would have been some redistribution of wealth. Quakerism, Fox explained, was opposed to those who 'have long cumbred the ground'; 'such are harlotted from the truth, and such gets the earth under their hands, Commons, Wastes and Forrest, and Fels, and Mores, and Mountaines, and lets it lye wast, and calls themselves Lords of it, and keeps it from the people, when so many are ready to starve and begg'. 'You wallow your selves in the earths treasure like swine in the mire', Nicholson told the gentry, 'and never consider that the earth is the Lords . . . and that he hath given it to the sons of men in general, and not to a few lofty ones which Lord it over their brethren.'[60] In 1659 Fox suggested that old monastic properties and glebes should be given to the poor, that 'great houses', churches, even Whitehall, should be converted into alms-houses.[61] (Benjamin Furly was later to advocate that a form of income tax could finance hospitals, free-schools, and alms-houses.[62]) Those who 'are taught of Christ' must make themselves 'equall with them of the lower sort'.[63] This statement reveals more than it intends. The Quakers were not communists: they probably had in mind a nation of small producers, with some limitations on the accumulation of wealth.

Quaker political allegiances were relatively uncomplicated. The civil wars, according to George Fox the younger, had been fought between (on one side) those 'accounted the wisest, richest, noblest and stoutest men' who 'did glory in their Wisdome, Riches, Nobility . . . and vaunted themselves over them that were made of the same Blood', and (on the other side) the 'contemptible Instruments, (as to outward appearance) as in Tradesmen, Plough-men, Servants, and the like, with some others'. The Quakers left no doubt that they were against 'the tyrannicall Kings and bloody Bishops'.[64] The Revolution had gone smoothly with the execution of the King, destruction of episcopacy, and abolition of the House of Lords. But it had halted midway, with, Fuce seems to suggest, the defeat of the Levellers at the end of the 1640s.[65] Cromwell had been God's instrument, and, despite some complaints, Quakers served in the Protector's commission of the peace and in the Army and Navy until they were purged. Though far from satisfied with the Protectorate, the Quakers would do nothing to bring it down if it meant the return of the Royalists.

Yet Quakerism is devoid of any coherent and identifiable political philosophy. Their attachment to parliamentary democracy varied, as did that of many of the radicals at this time. Some Quakers were willing to use the parliamentary system and to argue for greater democracy in the form of annual parliaments and rationalization of the electoral system.[66] When in 1659 republican agitation in the Army did bring down the Cromwellian regime, Quakers declared their willingness to serve the republican cause, with some it seems taking up positions in the militia and Army. But there was also a tendency in 1659 to support intervention against Parliament if it looked like furthering radicalism. According to Francis Howgil it was no crime to remove parliaments when they 'will not hearken to the cry of their Masters [the People]'.[67] Fox the younger condemned the parliamentary system as the agency of the propertied and suggested instead a benevolent dictatorship, acting on behalf of the people.[68]

v

The Quakers of the 1650s were not consistent pacifists. True, some do seem to have reached the pacifist position before 1660. But most were either concerned with stressing the peaceful nature of the movement rather than its opposition to the use of force under any circumstances (the distinction is important), or they were making statements approaching that of Burrough who told those in power in 1659 that if they would 'establish Righteousnesse' they were assured of Quaker support: 'Oh then we should rejoyce, and our lives would not bee Deare to lay downe'.[69] As Alan Cole pointed out some time ago, there was both ambiguity and lack of unanimity on the question of pacifism.[70]

We can see an excellent example of ambiguity in the case of the Quaker leader George Fox. His attitude towards the use of military force oscillated between his engagement to Cromwell denying 'the carrying or drawing of any carnall sword against any, or against thee Oliver Crumwell', and his proud report of the belief that a Quaker soldier was worth at least seven men.[71] Indeed, while he was not enthusiastic about the fact that some Bristol Friends had joined the militia in 1659, he did not condemn them: 'there is Somthing in ye thing', '& you cannot well leave them Seeing you have gone amongst them'.[72]

Some Quakers did seem to reach the pacifist position before 1660. When he became a Quaker John Lilburne found that the occasion 'of all outward wars, and all carnal buslings' had become 'in a very large measure . . . dead or crucified within me'.[73] William Dewsbury's light within led him, in 1659, into an anarchistic stance, saying (according to John Harwood) that 'there should not be a man in Israel to rule one over another, but that the rule and authority of man should be overturned, & Christ alone rule in the hearts and spirits of his people'.[74] There are also vague suggestions of pacifist notions among some of the Quaker soldiers in Scotland.[75]

But against this can be set the unwilling removal of Quakers from the Army at the time of George Monck's purge of his forces – for subversive principles, not refusal to fight – and the resultant protests of leading Quakers: 'have you not turned some of the Souldiers out of the Army, who have jeoperded their lives in the time of the gretest straits in the high places in the field?'.[76] Against evidence of certain Quakers' eschewal of violence can be placed the reality of a Quaker presence in the armed forces and the militia in 1659, Fox's later admission that 'some foolish rash spiritts yt came amongst us were goeinge to take uppe armes', and Burrough's statement, quoted above, referring to the laying down of Quaker lives.[77]

It is true that the Quakers always believed that the ultimate battle was spiritual. Utopia could only be created by the working of the spirit or light within upon the hearts and consciences of men and women. The kingdom would come, a Quaker explained to the Fifth Monarchists, 'not by an outward visible shining body, quelling and over-awing the enemies of his Kingdom, but by his inward and invisible Power in the hearts of his People'.[78] But force was by no means precluded. As Cole has pointed out, Fox recognized that 'the outward sword might have its place in fulfilling God's purposes on earth'.[79] The Quakers were not pacifist in any modern sense of the term. 'I am given to beleve, yt there is some great worke to doe by them, in ye nations, wth their outward sword, & yt time is not long till a good thing may bee accomplished by our English Armie', Burrough wrote in May 1659.[80] In 1660 George Bishop printed a letter he had written to Cromwell several years before, berating the nation's timidity. 'Did thy Sword (till of late) ever return empty from the blood of the slain, and the spoil of the Mighty[?]' he demanded of the Protector. The people of England, once magnificent in their belligerence, had become 'dead at the heart, lumps of flesh, and averse to War'.[81] Both Fox and Burrough talked in terms of a Protestant conquest of Rome.[82]

It is not until 1661 that we get, in Hill's words, the first 'official declaration of absolute pacifism in all circumstances'.[83] Before that time it is impossible to talk, as it is later, of the Quakers as a predominantly pacifist group. Self-preservation after the restoration of the monarchy in 1660, disillusionment with the effectiveness of political action, encouraged them to project their pacifism backwards. 'Pacifism was not a characteristic of the early Quakers: it was forced upon them by the hostility of the outside world.'[84]

VI

As we have seen, the Quaker critique of contemporary society and politics was not confined to polemic; and it is worth finishing this chapter by emphasizing this point. Action against oppression, in its various forms, was vital for Quakers just as it was for Levellers and Diggers. W!.ether symbolic protest or economic agitation, the emphasis was on action. It was what the Leveller Richard Overton would have called 'Practical Christianity'.[85] By your actions you are 'brought to the touch-stone', wrote the Quaker William Tomlinson, '*Your works, Your works*, they are your discovery'.[86]

Quaker activism expressed itself in various forms, most of which have been touched on already. We can see it in their opposition to tithes during the 1650s in parishes throughout the nation. Quakers, it was complained with almost monotonous regularity, were among the hard core who had 'not onely refused to pay any manner of Tythes . . . but doe pswade others to wth draw & substract their Tythes likewise'; 'givinge out in speeches that now noe tythes, duties or customary payments for tythes in any kinde are not due nor ought to be payd at all. . . And thereby have alsoe diswaded divers others . . . from paying of any tythes'.[87] Their 'main drift', as a petition from Westmorland put it, 'is to ingage the people against the Ministery by reason of Tithes'.[88] We know that during the 1650s at least a thousand Quaker resisters were proceeded against for their refusal to pay tithes; and it is likely that this figure is something of an underestimation of the true extent of resistance. Unlike the Levellers, the Quakers were willing to respond to this particular agrarian grievance, although as I have argued elsewhere the main impact of their campaign was psychological rather than economic.[89]

They also waged a guerrilla war against the clergy. Priests were interrupted or abused, and sometimes a Quaker would get to the church before the minister and address his waiting congregation. The Sussex Quaker John Snashford interrupted a minister and when the offended party offered 'to return home' asked him 'if he would flye'.[90] 'Come downe, Come downe, thou painted beast come downe thou art but an hireling & deludest the people with thy lyes', Mary Fisher cried out in the midst of a sermon by the minister of the Yorkshire parish of Selby.[91] These are but two examples of what proved to be a remarkably widespread problem – nearly 400 cases of harassment that we know of, most of which found their way to the courts.[92]

The Quakers' refusal to remove their hats before social superiors and to acknowledge titles, their use of the words 'thee' and 'thou' instead of 'you', anticipated the French revolutionaries in affirming human equality.[93] Obsession with 'breeding', respect for him 'that hath a gold Ring, and fine Apparel', merely reinforced 'earthly Lordship, Tyranny, and oppression'. Quaker 'non-respect of persons' was a testimony against class exploitation.[94]

The cool, academic analyses of twentieth-century historians tend to rob mid-seventeenth-century radicalism of much of its passion and urgency. Indeed, one almost needs to resort to massive quotations or to reprints of prose to really convey the power, the sheer apocalyptic fervour, of the Revolution radicals.[95] But there is more to the story than the pamphlet literature, communication by print. For the Quakers, as Richard Bauman has put it, rhetoric was 'not simply a rhetoric of words, but a unified rhetoric of symbolic action'; and acts had a significance 'above and beyond' their 'immediate frames of reference'.[96] The Quaker 'thee' and 'thou' (Bauman's example) was a sign of Quaker rejection of the world; it was a declaration of human equality; it was also a conscious effort to humble, to hit at 'honour' – a 'fearful cut to proud flesh and self-honour'.[97] Going 'naked as a sign', we have also seen, operated at a number of different symbolic levels. Even silence was rhetorical: an inward mystical communion with God, beyond, above, mere words. The Quakers severed themselves from society. But in the 1650s they did not retreat from it. As new men and women, 'the people of God called Quakers', they set out to conquer the world, not to hide from it. 'Our work in the world is to hold forth the virtues of Him that hath called us. . . . We are . . . to be witnesses for God and to propagate His life in the world.'[98] Such doctrine was remarkably malleable. The Quaker dictate 'let your lives speak' could betoken withdrawal, quiet separation from the world; but it could also sound forth in more militant, clarion terms. The latter predominated in the 1650s.

PART II   RESPONSES

[Sir John Berkenhead], *The Four Legg'd Quaker* (n.p., 1659?), Bodleian Library, Wood 416 (70).

CHAPTER 3
The elite and the early Quakers

I

We have dealt with Quaker activity and ideology; but what of the movement's actual impact? Obviously the arrival of the Quakers in the 1650s brought mixed reactions. The young John Locke thought them 'madd or jugglers', worthy of mirth and derision rather than rancour.[1] Oliver Cromwell and his Council suggested that Quaker perversity arose from a defect in understanding rather than 'malice in their wills'.[2] Others were more charitable. Radicals like Henry Marten treated with contempt notions that Friends were disguised Jesuits.[3] Indeed, we have seen that Friends were sometimes able to count on influential support. Charles Fleetwood's family attended London meetings in the 1650s, as did the Earl of Pembroke. There were Quakers in Cromwell's household.[4] Yet if we had to weigh support against hostility, the scales would tip in favour of hostility and fear. Scottish Quakers were automatically excommunicated during the 1650s; an order of the Glasgow synod forbade Presbyterians to trade, employ or indeed associate in any way with a Quaker.[5] In some areas of Britain evidence of a man's Quakerism was enough to have him turned out of the Army, out of his home, to lose him his tenancy, even to have his vote disputed.[6] In New England it was enough for him to be disenfranchised, or for him and his female co-religionist to be fined, whipped, branded, mutilated, banished or executed.[7] The Quaker threat – it was seen as a threat – had to be faced at all levels of political power: in the Army, in the borough and county communities, and in London.

II

Quaker successes in the Army were perhaps predictable, for the New Model Army was an acknowledged breeding-ground for radical ideas. Garrison commanders were not always sympathetic, but Quakers got support during the 1650s from officers and the rank and file. Quaker letters and journals mention progress in garrisons in York, Bristol, Holy Island and Berwick-upon-Tweed (Northumberland), Lancaster, Carlisle, Chester, Kent, Northamptonshire, Norfolk, London, Shrewsbury.[8]

The Quakers were particularly successful in the garrison towns of Ireland and Scotland. The peak of Quaker activity in Ireland was in 1655 and 1656; and the sect enjoyed some influential support.[9] Colonel Nicholas Kempson (brother-in-law of the better-known Edmund Ludlow) encouraged Quaker settlement in Cavan, 'promising he would build a meeting-house and do great Matters to promote Truth'. The Governor of Cork, Robert Phayre, later to become a Muggletonian, was reported as saying that 'more is done by the Quakers than all the priests in the country have done in a hundred years'. The Governor of Kinsale, Richard Hodden, kept a Quaker to preach to his troops and even hinted to Henry Cromwell (Lord Deputy of Ireland) that he should encourage Quaker settlement.[10] We know of meetings and conversions, mainly of soldiers, in Cork, Kinsale, Youghal, Cashell, Limerick, Bandon, Londonderry, Belturbet, Cavan, Dublin, Galway, Wexford, New Ross, Mountmellick, and Kilkenny.[11]

A similar kind of success was reported in Scotland in 1657, again with support in high places. The order books of General George Monck, the commander of the regiments in Scotland, provide clues to Quaker penetration, for Monck was to purge Quakers from his army. Though not numerous – about forty Quaker soldiers were purged – Quaker converts were widespread. Three of his five regiments of horse were affected, five of his eleven foot regiments, and his regiment of dragoons. If Monck had not acted, the indications are that his forces would have become riddled with Quakers.[12]

Both Henry Cromwell (in Ireland) and George Monck (in Scotland) moved against what they perceived to be Quaker subversion of their regiments. Occasionally, it is true, military protection of Quakerism had brought conflict with the civilian population or even clashes between fellow soldiers, as at Limerick when officers and soldiers who were attending a Quaker meeting resisted the governor's troops when they attempted to break it up.[13] Yet it was probably fear of ideological contamination rather than a few sporadic outbursts of disorder which induced Monck and Cromwell to act. The Quaker soldier's refusal of the customary compliments due to a superior, and the Quaker officer's deeming of such compliments to be unnecessary, were certainly not conducive to military discipline. 'Our most considerable enemy nowe in our view are the quakers', Henry Cromwell wrote in 1656; 'I thinke their principles and practises are not verry consistent with civil government, much less with the discipline of an army.' Quaker insubordination reminded one of Monck's commanders of 'that factious temper of the army about the tyme the levellers appeared at the first'; 'the levellinge principle lyes at the bottome'.[14] Monck agreed. 'Truly I thinke they will prove a very dangerous people, should they increase in your army', he wrote in a letter to Oliver Cromwell, 'and be neither fitt to command nor obey, but ready to make a distraction in the army, and a mutiny uppon every slight occasion.'[15] So the ranks of the Irish and Scottish regiments were purged; Quaker officers were cashiered. In Ireland Quaker pamphlets were seized and burned. Visiting Quakers were apprehended and then banished from the island. Many were imprisoned: ninety-two were in gaol at one time or another during the years 1655 and 1656.[16]

III

There was great variation in the gentry's responses to Quaker penetration of the provinces. Influential radical support could stave off persecution and encourage Quaker growth. In Bristol in 1654, where in the words of Alan Cole 'the bulk of the Radical party were among the earliest converts to the new religion' (garrison commanders, a former MP, the wife of an assize judge, a high-ranking government bureaucrat), the Common Council was eager to rid the city of Quakerism but felt inhibited by the sect's influential allies. Colonel Adrian Scrope who was in charge of the Army in Bristol had said that 'if the Magistrates did put them [the Quakers] in prison one day, he would put them out the next'.[17] There is evidence of similar influences in Lancashire and Cheshire, mainly because of the presence – in the Lancashire quarter sessions and the Cheshire assizes – of Thomas Fell, whose widow was later to marry George Fox, and the regicide John Bradshaw. When Cheshire justices were attempting to crush Quakerism in 1655, Fell and Bradshaw were ordering the release of Quakers from prison. They were to do the same again in 1656.[18]

But examples such as those above (and there are one or two others[19]) were the exception rather than the rule. In Newcastle the Corporation, clergy, and Merchant Adventurers' Company all banded together to deal with the Quaker menace. Meetings were barred from the town and forced across the river to Gateshead; the employment of Quaker apprentices was prohibited.[20] When Quaker itinerants arrived in Norwich in 1654 they were promptly escorted back out of town.[21] In Chester, during the 1650s, a succession of mayors ensured, often quite brutally, that Quaker progress in this city would be limited.[22] Much the same happened in Plymouth,[23] Maidstone,[24] and Arundel,[25] to give a few more examples. Movement into small islands could be controlled too; when Quakers crossed to the Isle of Wight the governor sent them back to the mainland.[26]

My general impression, then, is that there was little reluctance to act against the Quakers. In fact in mid-1656 there was a concerted drive in several counties to limit the expansion of the movement. The Essex Quarter Sessions ordered the suppression of 'all unlawfull tumultous Assemblyes' and the arrest of all members of the sect found 'within this County wandring and haunteing from place to place'. Similar directions were issued by the courts in Devon and Cornwall, where watches were set up on highways and bridges 'for the preventing of this great contagion, that infects almost every corner of this Nation'. In Devon 'psons of estate' with 'sufficient weapons' were engaged to apprehend those 'styled by ye name of Quakers disaffected to ye psent govmt', and over a score of itinerants were netted in a matter of weeks.[27] Wiltshire and Somerset justices were urged by their grand juries to do something about 'the increase of persons known by the name of Quakers'.[28] Clearly Oliver Cromwell's policy of toleration was only what the local communities would make of it.

Quakers appeared before the quarter sessions and assizes for a variety of offences. A few were prosecuted under the Blasphemy Act of 1650.[29] Many were in trouble for disturbing ministers and disrupting church services, offences punishable either by an Act instituted in the reign of Mary (1 Mar. St. 2 c.3) or by the provisions contained in Cromwell's proclamation of 1655 which was specifically aimed at Quakers.[30] Several justices used the Vagrancy Act (39 Eliz.c.4), before its revision in 1657, bending the spirit if not the letter of the law in an effort to contain

Quakerism. North-country men and women were whipped out of southern towns.[31] Magistrates proved both flexible and imaginative in their interpretation and use of the law. In Plymouth in 1655 the Quakers Miles Halhead and Thomas Salthouse were prosecuted under Cromwell's proclamation against the provoking of duels.[32] There is evidence too that the oath of abjuration, intended for Catholics, was employed against Quakers in Oxford and Devon.[33]

At times the application of the law was somewhat shaky. An enquiry into the detention of Quakers by the Sussex authorities revealed that imprisonments had been illegal and the legal paperwork faulty. The affair had been one of religious prejudice.[34] We know that justices were tempted towards a certain lack of legal precision by an awareness that failing all else they would be able to detain a Quaker offender for contempt of court – for refusing to remove his hat, for example, or for saying in open court like Mary Fisher that 'all the gentlemen Justices & ministers on earth are theives & robbers'.[35] A committee of the Council of State was to suggest in 1658 that the hats of Quakers be removed before they entered court.[36]

IV

It is quite clear that there was growing discontent in the provinces, dissatisfaction with a central government which permitted groups like the Quakers to flourish. There were rumblings about official encouragement of radical sectarianism. Even Cromwell's proclamation of February 1655, which was aimed specifically against the Quaker practice of interrupting church services, was greeted with a certain amount of cynicism in some quarters. The minister of Earls Colne, Ralph Josselin, was to suggest (rather astutely) that 'perhaps the clause in his declaration not to disturbe the minister in exercise, was to hint to them, they might doe it after if they would, securely, for that is their practice'. When the young Quaker James Parnell died at the beginning of 1656 during a fast in Colchester gaol, it was rumoured that Charles Fleetwood, Major-General for East Anglia, had sent orders for his release which had arrived too late. Josselin's relief was symptomatic of the uncertainty: what a 'triumph his partie would have made' had the Quaker been freed.[37] In 1656 a single event, the Nayler episode, revealed these fears and tensions.

In October 1656, the year in which many had predicted that the millennium would commence, Nayler entered Bristol on a donkey, his hair and beard styled in the manner attributed to Christ. His companions, mostly women, walked beside him singing 'Holy, holy, holy, Lord God of Israel'. They kissed his feet and laid their garments before him in the mud. This symbolic entry, 'a sign of the second Coming of Christ' ('Thy name is no more to be called James but Jesus' wrote one of his followers), was the culmination of a triumphant procession through Somerset after his release from a period of incarceration in Exeter prison. The Quakers were promptly arrested and eventually sent to London where Nayler was examined by a parliamentary committee. The adulation continued during his detention. One follower, Dorcas Erbery, a daughter of the radical William Erbery, repeated her claim that she had been dead for two days and that Nayler had resurrected her; others continued to kneel before him.[38]

The reaction of MPs was intense. The debating continued throughout December and raised questions both legal and constitutional; indeed the whole issue of the respective powers of Protector and Parliament. The nation's image was threatened. 'Consider how you stand in the opinion of the world', the Master of the Rolls warned the House. MPs were shocked by the extremity of the offence, the audacity of the 'blasphemy'. 'He that sets himself up in Christ's place', proclaimed the rigid William Boteler, 'certainly commits the highest offence that can be.'[39] But above all (as Christopher Hill has pointed out) it was the Quaker movement and the government's religious policy that were in the dock.[40]

The outburst revealed real concern at the dramatic increase in Quaker numbers. 'These vipers are crept into the bowels of your Commonwealth, and the government too', explained one member; 'They grow numerous, and swarm all the nation over; every county, every parish.' Nayler was a leading Quaker, some said *the* leading Quaker, so it was an ideal opportunity to demonstrate the effectiveness of savage punishment as a deterrent. 'Cut off this fellow, and you will destroy the sect', Dennis Bond argued. Richard Cromwell told the diarist Thomas Burton that he was convinced Nayler 'must die', and there were Mosaically inspired suggestions of stoning. Others were less certain of the political wisdom of providing the movement with a martyr, though they agreed on the need for 'some endeavour to suppress the growth of them in general'.[41] Some were worried about creating an ambiguous precedent which might later be used against MPs themselves: 'We may all, in after ages, be called Quakers.' There were voices for moderation – John Lambert's was one – and Cornelius Holland, an MP with previous Leveller connections, spoke bravely for liberty of conscience. 'The opinions they hold', thought Colonel William Sydenham, 'do border so near a glorious truth, that I cannot pass my judgment that it is blasphemy.' Yet even the more moderate were worried, like Oliver Cromwell, about the Quaker threat to the 'civil peace'.[42] In the end, the death penalty was defeated (narrowly: by 96 to 82) and a more 'lenient' punishment settled upon. Nayler was to be branded, bored through the tongue, whipped, pilloried, and humiliated. He was then to be confined, indefinitely, without outside contact and at hard labour.[43]

The Passion of Nayler continued with his punishment at the pillory near the Royal Exchange in London. A contemporary pamphlet described the proceedings. Nayler's female followers gathered around him; one behind, two at his feet 'in imitation of Mary Magdalen and Mary the Mother of Jesus, and Mary the Mother of Cleophas, John 19.25'. A placard proclaimed 'This is the King of the Jews'. Its writer, Robert Rich, sat nearby, singing softly, stroking and kissing the wounded Quaker and licking the brand on his forehead.[44] But the authorities had the final say, for three weeks later Nayler was paraded through Bristol facing backwards on a horse: a symbolic and humiliating reversal of his triumphal entry.

v

Stiffer legislation came with the aftermath of the Nayler affair, partly because of pressure from the provincial gentry, partly because Cromwell was the good constable. Cromwell's religious policy had been under attack during the Nayler debates. Critics bemoaned the 'sad effects of Toleration'. 'These Quakers, Ranters, Levellers, Socinians, and all sorts', complained Major-General Skippon, 'bolster themselves under thirty-seven and thirty-eight of [the Instrument of] Government.' 'I heard the supreme magistrate say, "It was never his intention to indulge such things"; yet we see the issue of this liberty of conscience.' Major-General Goffe agreed. 'I shall not entertain an irreverent thought of *The Instrument of Government*. I shall spend my blood for it. Yet if it hold out anything to protect such persons I would have it burnt in the fire.'[45] In the aftermath of the Nayler affair petitions from Northumberland, Durham, Newcastle, Chester and Cheshire, Bristol, Cornwall, Devon and Exeter pressed Parliament to take action against the Quakers.[46] Concessions would have to be made. As Cromwell had been advised earlier, 'the Parliament will take order about them If your Highnes will give leave'.[47]

In May 1657 the Protector gave his assent to the Petition and Advice which narrowed the limits of toleration set out by the Instrument of Government, its predecessor and the initial charter of the Protectorate. In June, with the Quakers in mind, Parliament extended the old Elizabethan Vagrancy Act. The new version gave justices or officers of corporations *carte blanche* to move against 'all and every idle, loose and dissolute person and persons . . . found . . . vagrant and wandring from his or their usual place of living or abode, and shall not have such good and sufficient cause or business for such his or their travelling'. It was this question of definition, 'these *terminis generalibus*', which worried some MPs. 'If you leave it in the power of justices to judge who shall be wanderers, for ought I know I myself may be whipped.' But the critic, Major Audley, did not balk at the statute's use against Quakers: 'I could freely give my consent that they should be whipped.' Originally proposed stipulations of distance, allowing wandering of up to ten miles, were rejected by the House. Stipulations of wealth were not even discussed. All depended upon the vagaries of local justices; they had a weapon to restrict movement not only from county to county and parish to parish, but within the parishes.[48]

Parliament also passed (in June 1657) an Act for better observation of the Lord's Day. The Act provided for a maximum fine of five pounds or six months hard labour for disruption of ministers. Attendance at church became compulsory once again – at church or other 'meeting-place of Christians', but the latter had to conform to a new definition of 'Christian' which excluded Quakers. Quakers could now be prosecuted for not attending church. The half-a-crown fine seems small, but it was roughly equivalent to the weekly wage of a labourer. Quakers could also be fined ten shillings for travelling on the sabbath.[49]

Justices made use of their increased repertoire. The law against vagrants was made only for Quakers, an Ipswich JP told the Quaker George Whitehead; and it was used against the sect in Suffolk, Somerset, Devon, Wiltshire, and Dorset. Sometimes the offenders were taken only a matter of three or four miles from their homes. They were often men of substance, merchants or tradesmen combining economic and spiritual business. It would be tedious to relate examples, but the case of John Evans, a wealthy Englishcombe yeoman taken at Plymouth in November 1658 and whipped back to his Somerset home, was not untypical.[50] The Lord's Day Act had some impact as well. A few Quakers were presented for not attending church, in Cornwall, Suffolk, Essex, and Northamptonshire.[51] Justices in Gloucestershire, Devon, Essex, Suffolk, and Yorkshire prosecuted other members of the sect for profanation of the Lord's Day (usually by travelling on the sabbath).[52] Some felt that the political climate permitted a tougher line. Thus in Devon in 1658 the Court of Quarter Sessions ordered that Quaker itinerants be apprehended and their books burned.[53]

VI

Why were the governing classes so worried by the inroads of Quakerism? Edward Butler, MP for Poole, explained his fears. Quaker 'principles and practices are diametrically opposite both to magistracy and ministry; such principles as will level the foundation of all government into a bog of confusion'.[54] Many others shared his alarm. There was, quite simply, fear of social anarchy.

It was an age in which people were convinced of the power of ideology – a conviction only reinforced by the events of the 1640s and 1650s. Religion was the 'foundation of government'. It is 'hard to be doubted', wrote Charles Davenant in 1698, many years after the period with which we are concerned, 'but that if the common people are once induced to lay aside religion, they will quickly cast off all fear of their rulers'.[55] Presbyterian and Anglican alike stressed the political and social necessity of their brands of orthodoxy. 'If there was not a Minister in every Parish, you would quickly find cause to encrease the number of Constables.' 'It is the duty of all good Christians to be meek, gentle, humble, patient, obedient to superiors'; and it is 'the duty of all good Pastors to exhort their people to the practise of these and the rest of the fruits or graces of the Spirit'.[56]

Early modern England was a society 'classed by subordination', and the patriarchal doctrines of the state were imbibed (in theory at least) from the cradle onwards. Children, servants, and apprentices who understood their status in the household needed little political sophistication to grasp that the same applied to their place in the state.[57] As the New England catechism put it, by honouring thy father and mother the fifth commandment had in mind all superiors, 'whether in family, school, church and commonwealth'.[58] Status and rank were reflected in manners, speech and dress.[59]

But the Quakers rejected the hegemony of the elite. They questioned the primacy of the Scriptures, rejected the need for an established church or ministry, and challenged the rigid hierarchical structure of society. When they talked to superiors Quakers used the egalitarian (possibly northern[60]) 'thee' and 'thou' instead of 'you', thus breaching the social etiquette of discourse. They refused to recognize titles, to bow or to doff hat. In their own dress (plain dress) they threatened the conventions of social distinction.[61] They even permitted their women to preach; a 'monstrous' practice, 'condemned as against nature'.[62]

It is difficult for us to imagine the sheer horror experienced by many of the elite when confronted by the socially iconoclastic Quakers. Full of impudency and 'no woman but a man' was how one justice's wife described the Quaker Ann Blaykling.[63] Such 'huswives as shee was', Deborah Maddock was told by the Mayor of Chester, were 'fitter for the Stockes or to bee ducked in an Cooke-Stoole than carry Letters; and come soe before her Betters so irreverently'.[64] 'Sirrah', Thomas Ellwood's gentry father responded when his Quaker son used the plain language, 'If ever I hear you say Thou or Thee to me again, I'll strike your Teeth down your Throat.' And when Thomas stood hatted before him, Ellwood senior smote his son with 'both his Fists'.[65]

'Such as now introduce Thou and Thee will (if they can)', Thomas Fuller warned in 1655, 'expel Mine and Thine, dissolving all property into confusion.'[66] 'My Lord, the whole world is governed by superiority and distance in relations', wrote a colonel in Monck's forces in 1657, 'and when that's taken away, unavoydably anarchy is ushered in.'[67] Quaker principles, Charles II was to urge, were 'inconsistent with any kind of government'.[68] As early as 1653 there was talk of 'those new Antichristians . . . who are not free to be Tenants to other men';

and Lord Conway, whose wife was not unfriendly towards the
sect, thought that the design of the Quakers was to 'turn out the
landlords'.[69] The gentry and ministers were alarmed by the sect's
effect upon the common people. The Quakers were involved in
an intransigent and property-threatening campaign against tithes.
They stirred up the people against lawful authority and tempted
the lower orders with dangerous doctrines. 'O how did this take
with the vulgar sort', wrote Lord Saye and Sele shortly before the
Restoration, 'when they thought they should enjoy that liberty,
as to be under no rule, no reverence to be given either to
Magistrate or Minister, Parent or Master . . . and this was it that
made it so easily embraced, and so suddenly spread it about the
Kingdom.'[70]

This stress on the perceived threat to patriarchalism does not
mean that other factors are unimportant when it comes to
explaining elite attitudes towards the early Quakers. We need not
doubt the extent of the outrage that was provoked by the
Quakers' theology: their minimization of the importance of a
historic Christ, their belief that the spirit was above the
Scriptures, their rejection of orthodox ideas about the Trinity and
Heaven and Hell.[71] The battle for souls was genuine enough.
'While thousands are in damnation for want of the light, they
would take it from you, that you might go there also', Richard
Baxter wrote of the sects in 1657, and he obviously had the
Quakers in mind.[72] It was 'eternal Salvation' that was at stake.[73]

Nor should we underestimate the way in which anti-
Quakerism and anti-Catholicism merged in the ever-appealing
and powerful myth of 'Jesuits in disguise'.[74] It was an accusation
levelled at most sects at one time or another, but one which seems
to have been used most frequently against the Quakers.
Franciscans, Jesuits, Capuchins – the argument ran – had
disguised themselves as Quakers in order to undermine church
and state. 'Thus these Papists have begotten this present Sect of
Quakers. . . . And so you have here and there a Papist lurking to
be the chief Speaker among them', wrote Richard Baxter in
1655.[75] And his convictions were shared by William Prynne,
Edmund Calamy, Marchamont Nedham, Lord Saye and Sele, Sir
Justinian Isham, Jeremy Ives, John Tombes, Immanuel Bourne,
Henry More, Oliver Heywood, and many others.[76] For
Calvinists the sect's emphasis on 'mans free-will' and their denial
of predestination seemed to smack of popery. Their light within

appeared but a guise for the Catholic doctrine of grace. Veneration of poverty, fasting, visions and revelations, 'extolling of Monasticall Community and Virginity', the sect's calls for toleration, led those in power to detect (with a little imagination) the 'hand of a Jesuit . . . in the Quakers Religion'. William Prynne noted that the sect hailed from Lancashire and Westmorland, notorious country for papists. Their refusal to take the oath of allegiance and supremacy and to abjure papal authority was surely tangible proof of their duplicity rather than evidence of Puritan scruples over oaths. Their meetings were obvious nurseries for Catholicism.[77]

It was the classic conspiracy theory. Rome was out to destroy Protestant England by any means at its disposal, even through the agency of sectarianism. Once this hypothesis was accepted then all fell into place, all evidence seemed to support the original contention: on moral, theological, political, and geographical grounds. The Quaker movement was new, its doctrines vague or unknown; and it was easy to explain the unfamiliar, the incomprehensible, the apparently threatening, in familiar, comprehensible, readily identifiable terms. Hysteria, the sociologists tell us, is the redefinition of the ambiguous and uncertain into the generalized and absolute so that people at least know what they fear.[78] So it was with the Quakers, who, like the Catholics, were seen as a potential fifth column. 'Its a wonder to see how they multiplie; and its to be feared those Croaking Frogs, the Priests and Jesuits, under this Cover of simple Quaking, steale away the peoples hearts from subjection [a]nd obedience to Government', the newspaper the *Publick Intelligencer* commented in 1656.[79] By advocating toleration and undermining the established institutions of church and state, Quakers were at the very least discrediting Protestantism so that the papists would be able to say, 'see now what it is to depart from the Unity of the Romane Catholike Church'.[80]

VII

During the Interregnum, then, there was, for one reason or another, considerable hostility towards Quakers. We have seen that this tension helped to intensify dissatisfaction with the Cromwellian regime, forcing a more conservative religious settlement. In Kent, for instance, the Quaker issue was splitting the radicals and giving a boost to 'the re-emergence of political moderation'.[81] All this had happened by 1658. But it was in 1659 that the real impact of anti-Quaker feeling was felt. We shall return to this in chapter 5.

CHAPTER 4

Popular hostility towards Quakers

I

Like the elite, ordinary people varied in their responses to the early Quakers. The movement's success during the initial decades of its existence, and what is known of its social composition, suggests that the Quaker message was able to attract substantial numbers of what were known as the middling and poorer sort of people. There is evidence too, at the popular level, of community support of Quakers, particularly over the sect's vehement opposition to tithes. As George Whitehead observed from the vantage point of the early eighteenth century, tithes had 'set tender People' against the priests and gentry so that Quaker numbers 'the more increased'.[1] When a Quaker labourer was imprisoned in 1658 for small tithes the townspeople of Leverton in Lincolnshire paid the amount due and he was freed. In Bedfordshire in 1657 community pressure persuaded a minister to return goods seized from a Quaker for non-payment of tithes. Neighbours might warn a Quaker of approaching constables. They might, as the Wiltshire and Somerset sufferings suggest, harvest his crop for him while he was in prison. The Exchequer records sometimes betray evidence of sympathy. There are the occasional cases which imply that tithe owners had great trouble either in proving a claim or in determining the actual yield of their debtors – simply because it was impossible to get witnesses.[2]

Nor were local office-holders immune. Four Herefordshire constables turned Quaker in 1656, and there are several cases during the 1650s – from Cumberland, Yorkshire, and Somerset – of constables and tithing-men refusing to serve or execute warrants on erring Quakers.[3] In an incident in Berkshire in 1665 a minister was unable to locate the local constable to break up a Quaker meeting because he was actually at the meeting.[4] Keith Wrightson has demonstrated that in early modern England such local officers were mediators or 'brokers between the demands of their governors and those of their neighbours'. They often sided with local needs rather than the law if it guaranteed a minimization of conflict within the community.[5]

So there is evidence, as indeed one might expect, of sympathy at the village and parish level, something that (as we saw in the previous chapter) alarmed the men of property. But there is also a great deal of evidence for the opposite, for popular hostility towards Quakers. The issue is less clear-cut than it is for the attitudes of the elite. Yet my impression is that the end result was much the same; that it would still be true to say that the general reaction towards the early Quakers was one of hostility and fear – at all levels of society.

II

There are many examples of popular hostility towards Quakers. During the early years of the movement missionary activity was invariably accompanied by unrest and hostility. In the villages and towns of Cumberland and Yorkshire in the 1650s, Quakers were frequently set upon by groups of assailants armed with staffs and clubs. In Lancashire, said George Fox, referring to his own unfortunate experiences, it was the custom 'to runn 20 or 40 people upon one man'. It was the same further south. In Bristol, in 1654, the apprentices were out in the streets calling for the sect's removal. In Evesham, in 1655, when they attempted to hold meetings Quakers were stoned, spat at, and urinated on.[6] We could go on; the mob attacks of 1659 and 1660 provide other obvious examples.[7]

But if easily established, popular hatred is harder to explain. The sources simply do not permit an analysis of victims and mobs in the way that George Rudé has done for crowd activity in eighteenth-century France and England.[8] There are no police files to work from; and since (significantly, it appears) the authorities rarely took action against the attackers of Quakers, the quarter sessions and assize records are seldom of much help. The Quakers rarely named their opponents or described the mobs, except in the vaguest of terms. There are frustrating gaps in the little evidence that is available: we may know who the victims of a particular incident were but not the attackers; we may discover Quakers engaged in activities which could be expected to provoke popular hostility – engrossing or hoarding of grain, for example – yet never link those Quakers to any specific incident.

Nor does the nature of Quaker offences permit an analysis of witnesses against Quakers in the manner that Alan Macfarlane has with witchcraft depositions.[9] Unlike many alleged cases of witchcraft, Quaker offences (disturbance of ministers, recusancy, non-payment of tithes) actually took place, and witnesses were usually ministers, churchwardens, constables or, during a slightly later period, professional informers. Yet, having said this, we do sometimes know either who the victims of crowd action were or the social status of the Quaker community in a particularly troubled area. The copious Quaker sufferings literature – the Quakers recorded all their trials and sufferings – often betrays valuable information concerning motives. Quarter sessions records and contemporary diaries are occasionally revealing. In short, we have enough to venture some suggestions.

III

Some of the hostility was overtly political. As Christopher Hill has observed, Quakers were attacked as 'Roundheads'.[10] 'It is the same man that was called Roundhead, that is called Quaker', wrote the Quaker Edward Billing in 1658.[11] This was the case in the days immediately following Charles II's restoration in 1660. Several Gloucestershire Quakers were manhandled when they refused to drink to the health of the King and 'the Confusion of all Phanatiqs' (a political as much as a religious soubriquet).[12] A Cambridge crowd chanted that the Quakers were 'rebels' and set about demolishing a meeting house. When Quakers were imprisoned in Lyme Regis in June 1660 a Dorset mob threw stones at the prison window. Others were attacked in Somerset and Essex.[13] When a Twineham labourer refused to join in with Restoration activities in Sussex because 'he did not know but that the Kinge maye bee killed within a small tyme', it was alleged that he was a Quaker.[14]

The Quakers were attacked as political radicals, identifiable remnants of the excesses of the Interregnum. As Arise Evans put it in 1660: 'The Quakers give out forsooth, that they will not rebel nor fight, when indeed the last year, and all along the War, the Army was full of them.'[15] Others must have shared his sentiments. Newsbooks and pamphlets reminded people of the military credentials of certain Quakers and attempted to link the sect with some of the more notorious figures of the Revolution.[16] Hugh Peter was said to have been sheltered by Quakers before his arrest.[17] George Joyce – alleged like Peter to have been Charles I's disguised executioner – was said to have turned Quaker and escaped to Holland.[18] A Welsh ballad proclaimed Quakerism a natural progression from soldiering: 'Y foru fe ae'n Drwper . . . A thrennydd yn Gwacer' (Tomorrow he becomes a Trooper . . . the day after that a Quaker).[19]

IV

Much of the hostility can be put down to simple ignorance, the effects of indoctrination from pulpit and pamphlet. Before he had even met any Quakers, Richard Davies was 'afraid of any who had the name of a Quaker'; they 'were much preached against' and were represented as 'a dangerous sort of people'.[20] Ignorance was nurtured by the propaganda of gentry and ministers, for the sect was portrayed as little more than a band of dangerous criminals and atheists. Readers of tracts, newsbooks, and the occasional almanac and chapbook were treated to tales of the bizarre effects of rejection of priestly and biblical mediators, the fruits of the Quaker over-emphasis upon the spirit within. There was 'a credible report' of the attempted sacrifice of children, accounts of the self-destructive antics of several Friends, allegations of witchcraft, incest, buggery, and general immorality.[21] Oft-repeated suggestions that Quakers were in reality a Jesuitical fifth column undermining the church and preparing the way for a return to Rome, pandered to a virulent anti-Catholicism.[22] Although we do not have any specific evidence for the popular image of the sect, what the ordinary person thought when he or she heard the name Quaker, we can get some idea from the dehumanizing anti-Quaker literature. While they may not have entirely swallowed the image of a secretly bloodthirsty sect, possessed of an unhealthy fondness for horses and a somewhat contradictory blend of asceticism and lasciviousness, who disparaged the Scriptures, threatened the stability of church and state, and were in all probability Jesuits in disguise, some of the muck – we have only to look at our own tabloid press – would have stuck. The popular image may also have included some vague historical awareness that in Münster, over a century earlier, fanatical principles not unlike those of the Quakers had led inexorably to levelling, bloodshed and anarchy; it was a comparison which the sect's enemies enjoyed making.[23] The image in print was damning enough; but when it is realized that many would have derived their sole knowledge of the new movement from word of mouth, by rumour, speculation, and from the hostile pulpit – or from the odd woodcut-print or ballad – it is not surprising that there was fear and hostility.[24] 'Some people were so blind and dark', wrote the Quaker Davies of the early years of his sect, 'that they looked upon us to be some strange creatures, and not like other men and women.' One man exclaimed when faced by members of the sect for the first time, 'these be Christians like ourselves, but where are the Quakers?'[25]

Even when the Quakers had already made their initial impact in a particular region there could still be hostility from outlying areas. Apart from normal class tensions in the local community and other factors which we will deal with later, the general rule seems to have been that it was outsiders who were attacked rather than close neighbours or members of the community. Thus in Lancashire in 1655 a meeting in Tottington was broken up by a 'deal of rude people' from nearby Bury. During the reaction against the sect in 1659-60 it was outsiders who were attacked in trouble in Newark-on-Trent and Broad Cerne. When the homes of local Quakers were mobbed there is some evidence that it was because they were sheltering aliens. When the Quaker John Coale preached in the streets of York in 1653, 'some of the Rude people of the Cittie did assemble at Night together, & Broke open the dores att Cornett Denhams . . . & sayd they would poole his wife in peeces for harboringe such a fellowe'.[26] Such findings are not surprising. The same was true of anti-Catholicism in seventeenth-century England and anti-Protestantism in eighteenth-century Toulouse.[27] It seems to have been parishes not noted for their Quakerism but adjacent to strongly Quaker areas that experienced the greatest paranoia during the Quaker fear in Cheshire and Lancashire in 1659: Manchester, Warrington, Cheadle, Chester, Bolton, Bury.[28] It was the idea of the Quaker that was hated and feared rather than the individual.

v

Xenophobia may account for some of the enmity. Seventeenth-century society was highly geographically mobile. The population turnover in a parish could be as high as 50 per cent in a ten-year period; and we can no longer assume that people lived out their lives in the same parish. *But* mobility was predominantly short-range, normally under twenty miles and to a great extent under ten miles. Even the majority of vagrants, who had wider geographical horizons than most of the population, travelled less than fifty miles from their place of origin.[29] Migration was intra- rather than inter-county. Indeed, in his survey of population mobility in seventeenth-century Sussex, Julian Cornwall discovered that only 14 of his sample of 202 predominantly rural inhabitants came from outside the county and that 9 of those were from adjacent Surrey and Kent.[30] In a more detailed study of Terling, an Essex village, Keith Wrightson and David Levine found that although it could be greater, the social arena of villagers was 'largely contained within a distance of ten miles'.[31] There was little contact between what we can roughly describe as North and South. A recent survey of vagrancy shows that only 4 per cent of vagrants taken in the south-east and south-west of England during the first half of the seventeenth century came from the North.[32] Of course there was long-distance migration to London. And in the provincial towns the population of outsiders would probably have been higher than in the villages. But even Peter Clark's figure for northern migration into the urban areas of Kent – 5 per cent of his sample of people resident in the town of Canterbury – is hardly indicative of an influx from the North. And in his work on seventeenth-century Maidstone Clark found that only 4 per cent of his sample had come from more than twenty miles away.[33] During the turmoil of the civil war years, with armies on the march, there was more mixing and travelling about. Yet it would still be true to say that the average villager, or for that matter many town dwellers, in the southern and Home Counties, the West Country or East Anglia, would have had few contacts with northerners. Edmund Skipp, a Herefordshire minister, did not even know where Kendal was.[34]

But the Quakers, most of whom during the earliest years were northerners (many of them women), were tramping about the countryside visiting the most remote and provincial of areas. In 1654 John Audland was averaging thirty miles a day, and visited at least forty places, passing backwards and forwards through more than twenty counties in a matter of a few months.[35] Unfortunately it is rarely that itineraries of this sort survive for this early period. But we do know that some time later (in the 1670s and 1680s) another northerner, Thomas Salthouse, covered nearly a thousand miles in less than six months.[36] Charles

Marshall (from Bristol) attended over four hundred meetings in thirty-six *different* counties during the first two years of his ministry.[37] There is no reason to assume that during the headier 1650s the pattern would have been very different. So it is at least possible that some of the hostility was a parochial reaction to what was seen as either an outside or northern invasion. Fear of Quakerism, Peter Clark has reminded us, was a fear of 'militant banded migrancy'.[38] According to Ralph Farmer, Quakers were 'Northern locusts', 'Morice-dancers from the North'.[39] 'Our quiet west country people do Judge them to be men of a strang humor', it was reported in 1655 after the sect's impact in that part of the country.[40] Quakers certainly met with intense opposition when they entered the rural areas of Sussex, which, we have seen, appear to have had little contact with outsiders.[41]

VI

Then there was the recurring accusation that Quakers were witches. The 'link' between witchcraft and Quakerism was noticeably strong in New England. Lyle Koehler has found that eleven of the twenty-two accusations of witchcraft made in Plymouth, Massachusetts, New Hampshire and Maine between 1656 and 1664 were directed at Quakers. And we know of a particularly nasty incident in 1656 in which two Quaker women accused of witchcraft were forced to undergo a brutal and humiliating internal examination.[42] In England there was an attempt by some Cambridgeshire ministers and justices to smear the Quaker movement with the charge of witchcraft. A Quaker widow, it was alleged, had changed an ex-Quaker into a mare and had ridden her 'four miles' to a 'midnight feast'. The case was brought before the assizes but dismissed by the judge.[43] There were murmurings about Quaker diabolism in Dorset in 1659 and 1660 which also seem to have come to the notice of the assizes.[44] Yet none of these charges received the complete encouragement of those in power. If they had, the history of the early Quaker movement might have been different: Cambridge might have become the Quakers' Salem.

None the less, the sketchy evidence that is available suggests that all talk of diabolism was limited to the elite: to priests and gentry. Lord Saye and Sele and the minister Joshua Miller spoke of the Quakers as the Devil's emissaries. They were that 'generation of Vipers, of late, by the power of Satan, sprung up amongst us'.[45] At the popular level, as with popular conceptions of witchcraft, there appears to have been little or no notion of the role of Satan in Quakerism. If he or she was seen as a witch it seems that the Quaker was perceived merely as someone with supernatural powers. Hence the aura of mystery shrouding the early movement. Hence the Quaker's place in the world of British folklore – similar to that of the Methodist over a century later.[46]

Quakers were said to bring the rain. It was thought that they had a Jonah-like effect if allowed on board a ship. And it was claimed that they bewitched their followers. After their conversions to Quakerism Richard Davies and his companions 'were not free to go into any neighbour's enclosures, for they were so blind, dark, and ignorant, that they looked upon us as witches, and would go away from us, some crossing themselves with their hands about their foreheads and faces'. Bewitching, it was argued, was performed either by means of charms – strings or ribbons about the wrists – or by getting people to drink from strange bottles, an allegation which seems to crop up fairly frequently. The rector of Siddington (Gloucestershire) refused a drink offered to him by a Quaker, saying that it was 'full of hops and heresy'.[47]

The case of the Quaker Jane Holmes, preserved in the Yorkshire assize records, provides us with a thumb-nail sketch of the speculation, uncertainty and superstition which could surround Quaker activity during the sect's formative years. When Jane arrived in the Yorkshire town of Malton in 1652 she was a disruptive influence: 'an instrument of the disturbance of the whole towne'. She abused the minister and drew people away from the church. She held meetings at strange hours of the night and caused divisions within families. Her enemies attributed some of her influence to a mysterious bottle which she was said to carry with her. One woman swore that she had seen the Quaker give a drink to a girl who thereupon lapsed into a trance. Another inhabitant, Anthony Beedall, claimed that he had met Jane and that she had told him that 'he had an evill spiritt within him'. She told him to follow her onto the Wolds and she would 'lye his sinns before him', so he accompanied her and drank from a bottle which she gave him. He went into a trance and was violently sick. But Jane said that it was only the spirit working in him and that if he would stay with her 'she would shew him Christ and his twelve

Apostles', and that if he would fast for forty days and forty nights 'he should be as good as Christ'. Finally, after an episode in which Jane allegedly advised him to walk across the Derwent rather than travel by a boat which she felt sure would sink, Beedall was found by friends. However, he admitted that he had 'had a great desire to goe to her againe'.[48]

George Fox himself was suspected to be something of a sorcerer or witch, who rode around on a big black horse and could turn people Quaker by merely holding them by the hands or by touching their foreheads. He was reputed to be able to read thoughts and 'discern the complexions of mens soules in their Faces'. Francis Bugg, an erstwhile convert who later became one of the sect's bitterest critics, said that it was 'the common Opinion' that Fox 'betwitch'd the People', and Bugg repeated rumours that the Quaker leader used to distribute groats to labourers who attended his meetings: 'those who took it and kept it, from that time fell into Trouble of Mind, and a restless Condition, and at last into Fits, and so became stiff Quakers: Others who carry'd him his Money again, or threw it away, were deliver'd, and recover'd their right State of Mind.' One tract even claimed that Fox had a long brush of hair by his ears like a fox's tail 'which he strokes often and playes with and sports with it'.[49] John Roberts was another Quaker who acquired something of a reputation as a wizard who was able to recover lost goods.[50]

The behaviour of certain sect members must have added to the mystery which surrounded the movement. William Mosse, a tailor from Over Whitley in Cheshire, linked his conversion to Quakerism to an incident in which, after a terrifying gallop on a big black horse, he was thrown over three great thorn hedges; 'since that time', Mosse explained proudly, 'he was enlightened'.[51] Fox, if his *Journal* is any indication, was not ashamed of his reputation and seems to have lived up to it – his bizarre leather suit, for example.[52] At least one contemporary noted that the Quaker leader had a tendency to fix his eyes firmly upon strangers 'as though he wold look them through'.[53] The Quakers' habitual meeting places in the early days – in woods, commons, on mountains, in houses 'most solitary and remote from Neighbours, situated in Dales and by-places' – encouraged speculation and stimulated a fear of the unknown. Malton observers talked suspiciously of the strange noises which emanated from the Quakers' nightly meetings.[54] Their trembling and shaking, behaviour traditionally associated with the work of Satan, what Lodowick Muggleton called their 'Witchcraft fits', must have seemed convincing testimony of demonic possession.[55]

Like the witch, the Quaker could be used to explain apparently inexplicable misfortune: such as the death of the parson in Sherborne in Dorset and the rapid exit of his successor.[56] They could be blamed for the tensions generated by a society in flux: for the break-up of families and the undermining of deference. And Quakers were readily identifiable, either as the outsider or the social nonconformist (with distinctive speech, behaviour and dress) in a tightly-knit community. Witchcraft could also explain the sect's otherwise unaccountable success.

VII

It is extremely difficult to explain what can best be described as the socio-economic basis for popular hostility. Some of the animus was probably economic in motivation. As anyone even vaguely familiar with corporation records will know, most communities were paranoiac about outside interference in local trade.[57] Since many of the early Quakers were traders, and since many combined spiritual with more worldly pursuits, commercial rivalry is a possibility which should not be ignored.[58] Edward Coxere certainly claimed that the hostile treatment he received in Yarmouth was due principally to competition over the herring traffic in which he was engaged.[59] Perhaps economic factors help to account for the rigid anti-Quaker legislation in many of the New England colonies in the 1650s – an area in which Rhode Island Quaker merchants seem to have been undercutting local trade.[60] It is also worth mentioning that the apprentice insurrection against Bristol Quakers in 1654 – merchants and shopkeepers – had the sanction of the boys' masters, probably the Quakers' business competitors.[61] But these are only suggestions.

The obvious approach when dealing with underlying social tensions and the motives behind popular hostility is to look at the composition of the mobs themselves. What sort of people attacked Quakers? Unfortunately, we have only Quaker descriptions to go on: 'Some of the very basest sort', 'the rudest sort of people', 'Rude people', 'the rude multitude', 'rude rabble', 'rude people of ye baser sort', 'rude people of ye town', 'Barbarous rude people', 'vile fellows of ye rude multitude',

'Scholars, lewd Women, Townsmen & Boys', the 'Rabble of Boys and rude people', 'scholars', 'youths', 'prentices', 'rude boys', 'prentices with the rude people'.[62] These descriptions are hardly the stuff that sociological analyses are made of, yet they are suggestive – if for the moment we can disregard the scholars, students of Oxford and Cambridge, who were involved partly as pranksters, partly as custodians of the social, cultural, and occupational *status quo*[63] – of two main groups. The first, though the descriptions may have been terms of abuse rather than sociological observations, was the lower orders. (The epithets 'base' and 'rude' were used frequently in the seventeenth century to describe the lower classes.[64]) The second group was the youths and apprentices.

The involvement of the lower orders suggests that the motivation behind some of the attacks on Quakers was the kind of social protest that George Rudé has found in crowd activity in the eighteenth century and others have discovered in popular violence in fourteenth-century Spain and sixteenth-century France: 'a groping desire to settle accounts with the rich, if only for a day, and to achieve some rough kind of social justice'.[65] Indeed, just as during the Gordon riots it was the properties of wealthy Catholics which were destroyed rather than those of Catholics in general,[66] there is a suggestion that it was sometimes the more substantial Quakers who were attacked rather than Quakers in general: Humphrey Bache the London goldsmith, Edward Billing the London brewer, Quaker merchants in Bristol.[67] In Colchester several of the sect belonged to the economic elite (and during the 1650s the political elite): John Furly junior and John Furly senior, linen draper and merchant respectively, the grocer Thomas Bayles, the baymakers William Havens and Solomon Fromantell. So they too would occasionally become the butts of a similar kind of class hatred – like that of the drunken feltmaker, for instance, who abused Furly senior and a companion, calling the latter 'a justless turd, old fool and old rogue' and saying that he (the irony obviously escaped the feltmaker) was as good a man as Furly's companion was; or that of the crowd of weavers and women who besieged the home of Furly junior in 1675, saying that they would 'pull Furly out by the Eares' and 'fire his house'.[68]

There are clues, too, in the occupations of Quakers. Some Lancashire Quakers were money-lenders.[69] We know that others elsewhere were dealers in the victualling trade – badgers, corn factors, millers, merchants, grocers, brewers, bakers[70] – so they presumably incurred that well-attested popular hatred and suspicion of middlemen and speculators, those who were generally thought to be the perpetrators of the periodic grain crises with which the nation was afflicted.[71] Some Quakers, then, were engaged in activity likely to incur popular wrath; but we only have firm evidence when they are actually caught and presented for such before the quarter sessions. Thus the Hertford grocer John King and (probably) the Bedfordshire yeoman John Crook (before he became a Quaker) were prosecuted for engrossing corn. The Walthamstow yeoman Mark Sarjeant was in trouble for regrating butter. The Colchester baker Arthur Condore was presented for selling underweight loaves.[72] When the Quaker Thomas Bush, a Sawbridgeworth maltster, was assaulted in 1659 by men armed with swords, clubs, staffs, and knives, it was not because of his faith but because he had used a false strickle for measuring grain. When the Colchester merchant John Furly was attacked during the weavers' riot of 1675 it was because he had been 'selling ye Corn out of ye land' during a time of dearth.[73] There is no evidence at this stage that other members of the movement were affected by the 'middleman' stigma, as would happen in the eighteenth century when food rioters attacked Quaker meeting houses because Quaker millers and corn factors had been engrossing and forestalling corn.[74] In the nineteenth century William Cobbett was to inveigh against Quaker involvement in the wholesale grain trade: 'They are, as to the products of the earth, what the Jews are as to gold and silver.'[75] But this lay in the future.

Finally, there are hints of some loose kind of organization in lower-class actions, perhaps a vague foreshadowing of the 'Skeleton Armies' of the nineteenth century, formed by members of the working class to combat the activities of the Salvation Army.[76] The weaver Samuel Wilde said that he frequented 'loose Societies and Clubbs' who encouraged him to bait the Quakers.[77] But, as with the students, this brand of anti-Quaker activity seems to have been mixed with drunkenness and revelry, though admittedly this tells us little of the original motivation.

The motives of the second group of assailants, the youths and apprentices, are equally difficult to determine. Both seem to have featured in attacks against the sect: in Bristol in 1654, in Dover in

1658, in London in 1659, and in London, Bristol, Norwich, Cambridge, and Wales in 1660 during the backlash at the return of Charles II.[78] We have seen, of course, that much of this hostility was political. Then there was what John Walsh has referred to as the hooligan element; the boys who attacked the Quaker meeting in London's Vine Street in 1659, for example, were said to have been plied with drink.[79] But these are not the only answers.

We know most about the apprentice riots in Bristol in 1654 and 1660. The unrest which began on 18 December 1654, with sporadic outbursts lasting into January 1655, was aimed solely at Quakers. A crowd said to be about 1,500 strong took to the streets, attacking meetings and the homes of Quaker shopkeepers and merchants; and a petition, demanding the removal of Quakers from the city, was presented to the Council. The situation was complicated. The apprentices drew upon a natural reservoir of anti-military feeling, feeling that had intensified with the Bristol garrison's blatant support of the Quaker movement during the sect's early days in the city. And there were the predictable cries for Charles Stuart. But for the purposes of our argument, three factors emerge: first, the allegations that the Bristol authorities supported the apprentices, if not actively then at least tacitly; second, the claim that Presbyterian ministers had incited the boys; and third, the report that the apprentices had the approval of their masters.[80]

The trouble in February 1660 was different. It was not aimed specifically at Quakers but was part of a more general reaction against decaying trade and the unrest of 1659 (an essential ingredient in the counter-revolutionary activity which heralded the eventual downfall of the Rump Parliament and the return of the secluded members and, ultimately, Charles II). Again the apprentices took to the streets, only this time they called for a free parliament and the preservation of the 'distressed Church' and condemned the heavy taxes which had been imposed upon their masters. But Quakers were attacked during the riots. They were forced to shut their shops. Some were threatened with death if they attempted to meet. They were generally treated pretty roughly.[81]

Why did the apprentices act? The role of their masters cannot be ignored, because they crop up in both episodes – though it should be noted that in 1660 some apprentices were beating their masters and forcing them to shut up shop, presumably as a form of enforced collective strike action. Likewise we should note the part played by Presbyterians. In fact in both 1654 and 1660 the apprentices were supporting the Presbyterian interest: the 'distressed Church'. It would of course be helpful to know exactly what sort of apprentices were attacking Quakers. Apprentices were a heterogeneous lot, sons of the gentry and yeomanry downwards and not strictly speaking of the 'inferior sort' or 'lower orders', the categories into which Rudé has rather carelessly lumped them.[82] Nearly 30 per cent of merchant apprentices in Bristol in the seventeenth century came from gentry families.[83] So we do not know whether they were acting as wage earners or the sons of the gentry. The little work that has been done, however, does suggest that youth groups and apprentices saw themselves as the custodians of social morality, and that they were ready to act as such against deviant behaviour, either by ridicule (charivaris) or by more direct means.[84] As Natalie Davis has shown, boys and youths in sixteenth-century France were allowed considerable licence in the games and festivities of the youth-abbeys (youth groups) as well as in the more serious religious riots; they were 'the conscience of the community in matters of domestic discord'.[85] The London apprentices, Steven Smith tells us, were uniquely well-organized, seeing themselves 'as moral agents, defending the right, whether it was the "right" Protestant religion, or the "right" behaviour of London's prostitutes, who were frequent targets of apprentice riots'.[86] Perhaps then it was as guardians not only of social morality but of the social order (as well as the 'right Religion') that the bands of apprentices and groups of youths took to the streets against the quarrelsome and socially disruptive Quakers.[87] This might also account for the allegations of official complicity, and for the role of masters and ministers.

VIII

Motives must remain speculative and vague. But what is clear is that outside direction, what Edward Thompson has described as the mob under 'magistrate's licence',[88] was an important feature of crowd attacks on the early Quakers. Again and again there are allegations of official involvement and complicity: in Sussex in 1657 and 1658; in Cornwall, Hertfordshire, and Nottinghamshire in 1659; in Cambridge in 1660.[89] When

Quakers were attacked in Bath in the 1650s they were told by one of their assailants that 'John Bigg the Mayor . . . bad them beat . . . Friends out of Town, because they were Quakers'.[90] In Bristol in 1654, though they issued orders for them to return to their homes, the local authorities made little effort to disperse the apprentices. It was even rumoured that one alderman, George Hellier, had said he would 'spend his blood, and lose his life before any of the Rioters should go to Prison'. When the troops eventually acted it seems to have been a unilateral decision.[91] When Quakers were set upon by a mob in Liskeard in Cornwall in 1659, 'some of the Rabble were Men of Figure, and one a Magistrate of the Town'.[92] As Thompson has pointed out, mobs could be extremely useful in an age without police forces. They could act for the *status quo* against intruders, disrupters, radicals. When George Rofe disrupted a church service which was attended by the Mayor of Hythe (Kent), the Mayor did not call for his officers but merely turned a blind eye while the Quaker was removed from the church and beaten severely by obliging 'vile fellows of ye rude multitude'.[93] The threat of popular action may also have been convenient for the Mayor of Macclesfield (Cheshire) in 1658. He warned visiting Quakers to leave his town; 'for ye maior said yt ye rud people of ye towne was redy to fall upon us & he could not rule them'.[94] It was the same sort of symbiotic relationship as that which existed between rulers and ruled in times of dearth, when middlemen became targets of mutual recrimination. Provided that it did not overstep the bounds, the mob could be a force for stability, and could be used against the Quakers, as radicals, much in the way that it was to be employed against the English Jacobins in the 1790s.[95]

Just as the local community had organized itself, as Clubmen, against outsiders in the 1640s,[96] it rallied against the Quaker threat. And mobilization was often directed, and occasionally led, by a local minister. As we shall see in the next chapter, it was from the pulpit that the anti-Quaker and anti-sectarian paranoia was whipped up in 1659. There are similarities to religious riot in France a century earlier.[97] We get the familiar ringing of church bells or beating of drums to rally resistance. In Crayke (Yorkshire) in 1653 it was the minister who organized resistance to the sect. The signal to rise was the tolling of the steeple bell, whereupon townspeople armed with clubs fell upon the Quakers. 'Corrupt Magistracies doe winke at the Evill doers', complained the Quaker Thomas Aldam.[98] When in 1657 members of the sect entered an unidentified market town in Sussex, a drum was beaten and the 'Barbarous rude people . . . Came marching up to the house Like men ready for battle'.[99] It was also to the beat of the drum that a mob armed with guns, clubs and staffs besieged a Quaker meeting in Broad Cerne in Dorset in 1660.[100]

Like the early Methodist ministers of the following century, the Quakers were men and women 'bent on removing traditional landmarks of social life', 'unleashing unwanted social and religious innovation'.[101] They could be extremely disruptive, splitting families (modern sects are hated for similar reasons) and upsetting the local community.[102] Indeed, sectarian loyalties could supersede familial ties, for, as one Quaker put it, 'it's better to forsake wife and children and all that a man hath . . . for christ and the truth sake'.[103] When Jane Holmes arrived in Malton in 1652 she drew women from their husbands and sons from their fathers. Thomas Dowslay's son told him he was no more to him 'than any other man'; and Major Bayldon was unable to 'keepe his wife at home'.[104]

Thus, attackers of Quakers can be seen as assuming clerical and magisterial roles: 'defending true doctrine or ridding the community of defilement'.[105] The Quakers were the objects of gut-conservatism as well as what John Morrill has called a 'fully developed provincialism', championed earlier during the 1640s by the Clubmen – Quakers occasionally referred to their opponents as Clubmen[106] – who had banded together to repel the invader and innovation. The Quaker was not only a 'foreigner' and intruder but also the very personification of the ecclesiastical and social upheaval so disliked by the provincial traditionalist who looked back nostalgically to the old order and (like the Wiltshire and Dorset Clubmen) the 'pure religion of Queen Elizabeth and King James'.[107]

IX

So popular animosity was a mixture of xenophobia, class hatred, and a superstition which merged with the world of witchcraft. It was stimulated and encouraged by indoctrinating anti-Quaker propaganda and by the behaviour of the sect itself. Quakers were hated as political radicals, as social and religious deviants, and in some cases as economic middlemen. In a sense, and almost paradoxically, the Quakers were a force for order. Despite the fulminations of those in power, fears that the Quakers would turn the world upside down, the sect's mere existence drew people together in defence of 'right' behaviour and reaffirmation of traditional values. Friends, in short, were a catalyst for popular traditionalism.

PART III   IMPACT

THE QVAKERS FEAR.
OR,

Wonderfull strange and true News from the famous Town of *Colchester* in *Essex*, shewing the manner how one *James Parnel*, a Quaker by profession, took upon him to fast twelve days and twelve nights without any sustenance at all, and called the people that were his followers or Disciples, and said that all the people of England that were not of their Congregation, were all damned creatures. Of his blasphemous Life and scandalous Death in the Jayl at *Colchester* this present month of *April* 1656. you shal here have a full Relation. The tune is, Summer time. Or bleeding Heart.

James Parnell,   The Quaker.

O God the Father of us all, (land
which made the Heavens, the Sea and
Assist us with thy holy Spirit,
And guid us with thy powerfull hand.

Let not the Devil our master be,
Who seeks our Souls for to devour,
But give us grace to arm our selves
That he of us may have no power.

A strange and true example here
I am prepared to declare,
Because that others may take heed,
And learn the living Lord to fear.

A man James Parnel call'd by name,
Committed hath such heynous crimes,
That very well he may be tearm'd
To be the wonder of our times.

He went about from place to place,
And undertook to preach and teach,
And matters he did meddle with,
That were too high above his reach.

The holy Bible he despised,
And was a Quaker by profession,
And said they all were damn'd to Hell
That were not of his Congregation.

Gods Ministers he set at naught,
And made disturbance up and down,
Where ever he did come or goe,
Both in the Countrey and the Town.

Yet many people followed him,
Which he did his Disciples call,
And they did believe what ever he said,
To be the truest way of all.

But for his wicked blasphemy
He apprehended was at last,
And unto Colchesters Jayl was sent,
And there in prison kept full fast.

Now while that he was in the Jayl,
He to the people thus did say,
That strange miracles would doe,
Before he parted thence away.

As Christ had fasted forty dayes,
And never at all did drink nor eat,
Nor in his body entred not,
So much as one small grain of Wheat.

So will I do James Parnel said,
Because you all shall know and see,
That I am a Prophet of the Lord,
And them that will believe in me

Shall have eternall joyes in heaven
Amongst the Souls whom God hath blest,
But those that will not me believe,
Shall never come where Saints do rest.

A many such blasphmous words
He to the people then did speak,
And twelve long dayes, and as many nights,
To fast he then did undertake,

CHAPTER 5

The Quakers, 1659, and the restoration of monarchy

I

Much has been written about the upheavals of 1659: we have a volume by Godfrey Davies and some excellent work by Austin Woolrych.[1] It is, I think, generally accepted that fear of radical sectarianism was a force behind the slide into briefly revived Presbyterianism and the return of Charles II.[2] Yet there is still a tendency in some textbooks dealing with the period to treat the troubles of 1659 as something of a postscript to what are seen as the more important tensions and events of the late 1640s and early 1650s.[3] Despite David Underdown's stimulating suggestions in *Pride's Purge* (1971), there has been little analysis of the panic of that year, of the mood which led many in the nation to look to the King, as Ralph Josselin observed, 'out of love to themselves not him'.[4] The subsidiary aim of this chapter is to stress the political importance of this single year, to put the emphasis back into 1659. Its main aim is to demonstrate the importance of one symptom of the unease of that year: the so-called Quaker threat. By all but the most radical, Quakerism became increasingly viewed with a mixture of alarm and hostility. Anxiety merged inexorably with reaction.

So the year was important for both the Quakers and the Revolution. In fact in 1659, as part of a more general fear of sectaries, hostility towards Quakerism persuaded many to look to the monarchy as the only salvation from social and religious anarchy. In other words, hostility towards the Quakers *contributed* to the restoration of the Stuarts.

II

The last year of the Interregnum was a time of great upheaval and radical excitement. In April 1659 republican and sectarian agitation in the Army finally brought down the Protectorate, and

in the following month the Rump of the Long Parliament was
restored. Dorothy White, a Quaker, proclaimed that God had
'come to turne the World upside down'; 'That that, which hath
ruled over may be brought down under, and that which hath been
of low degree, may be raised up by the power of God, to rule and
have the dominion'. 'The Lord Jesus Christ is come to reign',
wrote George Fox; 'now shall the Lamb and Saints have
victorie'.[5] With few exceptions, the Quakers were among those
who expected great things of the restored Rump and who
welcomed the revival of 'the Good Old Cause' in the Army. But
hopes that the Rump would create a Quaker utopia faded rapidly
as it became evident that sectarian demands would not be met.
'Alas, alas, this Glorious work of Reformation hath been
interrupted before our eye', Edward Burrough complained in
September.[6] Feelings of betrayal led many Quakers into open
acceptance of the Committee of Safety which replaced the Rump
in October, though not without reservations. 'Be less in words,
and more in action', Francis Howgil warned them.[7] The doubts
were justified, for tithes were not abolished, toleration was not
established, much-craved social and legal reforms were never
enacted. In December the Rump returned for a second time. By
early 1660 little hope remained: 'Where is the Good Old Cause
now?', asked Burrough, 'and what is become of it? in whose
hands doth it lie?'[8]

   Yet it had been a time of great hope for the Quakers as they
rehearsed and pressed home their political demands: the abolition
of tithes, the state church and the universities; religious
toleration; law reform. 'We look for a New Earth, as well as for a
New Heaven', explained Burrough; and the sect expected those
in power to secure this 'just freedom of the people'[9] Liberty of
conscience was what Quaker ex-soldiers (there were many of
them) claimed to have fought for. It was theirs 'both by Birth, and
dear Purchase'.[10] Anthony Mellidge, a Quaker naval captain, saw
such freedom, Leveller-like, as his right:

> We are not only free-born of England, but we have also
> purchased our freedome in the Nation, and the
> continuation thereof with many years hard service, the
> losse of the lives of many hundreds, the spoyling of much
> goods, and the shedding of much blood in the late war, by
> which at last the Lord overturned them, who then fought

> to enslave our persons, and infringe our liberty in the
> Nation, in the which liberty now, we do expect to
> worship God in spirit, and in truth.[11]

Ministers were warned that their end was speedily approaching. 'I know it appears to many of you, a thing very hard to be born', Burrough told Parliament; 'what? to forsake our godly Ministers think ye, to hear tell of laying them aside, is an amazement unto some of your minds?' But 'was it not the same concerning the King and Bishops?'[12] Quakers rode on horseback through the villages and towns of Westmorland, Cumberland, Lancashire, and Cheshire, collecting 15,000 signatures for an anti-tithe petition which they presented to the Rump in June. The following month saw another petition against tithes, this time signed by 7,000 Quaker women from throughout the nation.[13] The rich had gained from the Revolution the abolition of the Court of Wards: the poor and middling sort should be rewarded by termination of tithes. A king had been executed and episcopacy abolished, but still that hated tax remained: 'cannot he that hath delivered from the oppressive Court [of] Wards, and from the arbitrary Star-Chamber Court, from the hands of the late King, from the power of the Bishops, and from others . . . deliver out of the hands of this Philistine (the Tithes) also?'[14] Finally, the Quakers repeated their calls for law reform. George Bishop appealed to the General Council of the Army to 'smite' the lawyers. Quakers wanted lawyers removed, trial by jury, and Anglicization and codification of the law ('let all be drawn up in a little short Volumn, and all the rest burnt').[15]

Furthermore the Quakers expected to play a role in the events of 1659, and, in the words of Alan Cole, more than at any other stage in their development moved towards 'a militant revolutionary position'.[16] They were, as John Crook, Edward Billing, Dennis Hollister, Anthony Pearson, and other Quaker former justices and officers explained, neither 'uncapable nor unwilling' to serve their nation.[17] They demanded the restoration of all Friends purged from office because of their beliefs. They sent to London lists of Quakers eligible to sit as JPs.[18] And, as we shall see in due course, Quakers served in the militia, the Army, and probably in the volunteer regiments raised in August 1659 to crush the Presbyterian-Royalist risings. Burrough assured Parliament and Army of Quaker support provided they carried out the right reforms: 'Oh then we should rejoyce, and our lives would not bee Deare to lay downe'. Burrough also called for the setting up of a council composed of the various religious interests so that Quaker representatives could play an equal part in drawing up a solution for the civil government of the country.[19]

III

There was a growing feeling in 1659 that those in power had radical sectarian sympathies. Shortly after the recall of the Rump, the minister Richard Baxter received a letter relating with apprehension the change in government: 'Sr, such psons as are now at the head of affairs will blast religion if God prevent not'.[20] When the Rump reorganized the Army and set up the militia it was said that 'Levellers and expulsed Quakers' were being reintroduced.[21] The French ambassador wrote in June that Presbyterian ill-will 'compels the Government to put the arms of the country into the hands of the Sectaries, even of the Quakers, who up to this time had affected to seek nought but peace with liberty of conscience. The Spirit of God, by which they are ruled, now permits them to take part in the affairs of this world, and the Parliament seems inclined to make use of them.'[22] It was reported that in Ireland justices had been purged and replaced by Baptists and Quakers.[23] Fears intensified when volunteer regiments were raised in early August (in the wake of the Booth rising) amidst rumours of thousands of Quakers and sectaries in arms.[24] Sir Archibald Johnston of Wariston, a future member of the Committee of Safety, wrote in late August of his fear 'of the desseigne and indevour of som pairtye to putt the Anabaptists and the Quakers in airmes, which may theirafter be loath to laye doun their airmes, and to taik the advantage of this oportunety to take away the tithes and bring the maintenace of the ministery to hing at the belt of the State'.[25] People had not forgotten the episode of James Nayler, and his release by Parliament in September merely aggravated suspicions and convinced another Scottish observer, Robert Baillie, of the sect's 'Prevalencie'.[26] Sir Henry Vane was generally suspected of driving for a radical alliance with the sects as Henry Marten had been with the Levellers a decade earlier. Vane was said to favour Quakers; one, it was even rumoured, had anointed him king. He was thought to be an implacable enemy of the ministry.[27]

Fears also attended the setting up of the Committee of Safety in mid-October. 'We are all Quakers here', wrote John Locke, 'and there is not a man but thinks he alone hath this light within and all besides stumble in the dark.'[28] 'If Lambert succeeds the Church of England must fall', a Royalist proclaimed shortly before the dissolution of the Rump. There were rumours that the Army had interrupted Parliament 'to throw down the Ministery'.[29] Both Antoine de Bordeaux and the Scottish diarist John Nicoll thought that the Committee was on the verge of suppressing tithes. John Mordaunt claimed that they actually had. And Monck said much the same in justification of his march south.[30]

Of course the Rump's radical image was a distortion, for the majority of its members were not religious revolutionaries. It simply 'fell between two stools', pursuing a policy of conciliation of all, satisfying none; terrifying Presbyterians, while merely whetting radical appetites.[31] One of its first acts was to set up (on 10 May) a committee responsible for considering the cases of those imprisoned for 'conscience sake'. The committee arranged for the release of many imprisoned Quakers,[32] but still did not mollify the radicals. As George Bishop explained, by releasing tithe sufferers the Rump had recognized the injustice of the system, so how could they now retain tithes?; 'honest men every where' had had 'reasonable cause to expect their utter taking away'.[33] In May Quakers sent in lists of suitable and unsuitable justices, claiming later that they had been requested by Parliament.[34] Although they may have been entirely unsolicited, any rumours of the lists would have done little for the frayed nerves of the gentry.[35]

If sectaries were hopeful in the early days of the Rump, expectations were dashed on 21 May when the Rump declared its religious policy. Encouragement and protection of all who acknowledged the Scriptures as the revealed or written word of God, who believed in the Trinity and who did not disturb others in worship, fell short of sectarian expectations. Early in July, in an action clearly aimed against the Quakers, the Rump set up a committee to tighten the laws on disturbance of ministers. In October toleration was moved in the House, probably by Vane, 'but instantly decried'.[36] It was the same with tithes. A divided House declared for the tax on 27 June (though not before they had terrified clerical and propertied interests by even broaching the subject), on the very day that the Quakers had presented an anti-tithe petition of some 15,000 signatures.[37] 'The Quakers are not at all satisfied with this act', wrote Bordeaux, 'but it is more prudent to please the Presbyterians, whose number far exceeds that of all the other Sectaries put together.'[38] Judges publicized the vote when they went on their circuits. Nothing came of discussions of law reform. A bill was being prepared in June for correction of abuses by legal officers and the possible pruning of lawyers' fees, but it never surfaced. Edmund Ludlow alleged capitulation to the 'corrupt interests of the lawyers and clergy'. Such charges facilitated the overthrow of the Rump in October.[39]

We know very little of the internal politics of the government which replaced the Rump. Power still rested, unconcealed, with the Council of Officers. There was concern for the future of the ministry, universities, and college lands. And the Committee of Safety's vague declaration in early November for 'a Godly and learned Ministry', without mention of tithes, did little to dispel such doubts. But even if we do not believe Ludlow's allegations that legal and clerical interests bribed those at the top, it seems that the fears were exaggerated. As William Allen confided to Baxter in early November, 'I psum many of them not so little politicians as too farr to disoblige the ministery of the Nation by renderinge the continuation of their maintenance much doubtfull'.[40] One of the most interesting sources for the opinion of the officers is a report by the Quaker Richard Hubberthorne, a man who was usually well informed. He said that there had been a great deal of debate among the officers concerning tithes, with suggestions of reduction in the number of parishes and talk of a state-controlled ministry. The only hope for 'Lyberty and honest thinges', thought Hubberthorne, lay with Colonel Richard Ashfield, the inferior officers, Colonel Nathaniel Rich, and Vane. Rich declared to the Council that the Rump had done more for 'Lyberty of tender Consciences', and moved for another committee to examine cases of conscience; 'manny of them said it was good, but they put it of[f] and would not doe it'.[41]

Rumours of a radical religious settlement persisted. In December Monck was claiming that the Army had plumped for sectarian support with promises of tithe abolition. Ludlow, however, revealed the true temper of the Council of Officers; the Council decided that tithes would be retained, that any toleration would exclude 'the Quakers and some others, whose principles, they said, tended to the destruction of the civil society'.[42] It was probably during these debates that the Baptist Colonel William

Packer declared that 'before ye Quakers shoulde have there liberty hee woulde draw his sworde to bring in Kinge Charles'.[43]

Some must have feared that the radical sects would unite to force their own settlement.[44] Abolition of tithes, liberty of conscience, reform of the law, lawyers, and universities; here there was common ground between the Baptist Henry Denne, the Commonwealthsman Ludlow, the Quaker Edward Billing, the Independent William Sprigge, the Vanist Henry Stubbe, and the Fifth Monarchist John Canne.[45] Fifth Monarchists began to believe that rule by the saints was not rule by Fifth Monarchy Men alone, but by adherents to 'the Good Old Cause'. John Haggatt, a radical Independent, and the Quakers Bishop and Thomas Speed petitioned on behalf of suffering Baptists and Independents. Quakers organized an anti-tithe petition, signed by non-Quakers – for the 'free-born people of this Common-Wealth'. The Baptist Henry Denne and Vane's friend Henry Stubbe penned defences of the Quakers. Morgan Llwyd, a one-time Fifth Monarchist and Welsh mystic, urged 'liberty of conscience' for 'those that are called Quakers in scorn'. Stubbe actually advocated that the fearsome sect should sit on his proposed senate; and the Independent Samuel Duncon said something similar.[46]

No amount of parliamentary concession to the gentry and clergy could compensate for the fear unleashed by the Rump's formation of its militias in June and July. Parliament, wrote the Earl of Clarendon, 'had put the whole militia of the kingdom into the hands of sectaries, persons of no degree or quality, and notorious only for some new tenent in religion, and for some barbarity exercised upon the King's party'.[47] Sir George Booth said the same.[48] The radical Henry Stubbe agreed, though for different reasons; for him the only hope for the party for toleration was that it was 'possessed with the Militia of the nation, and under good commanders'.[49] Indeed it made sense that the Rump, distrustful of both Presbyterian and the uncommitted, should put power into the hands of the 'well affected'. But the Rump's actions added fuel to the very insurrection they were supposed to prevent. With its wide-ranging, emergency powers of detention of any suspicious person, its watch-dog role over impassive justices, its sectarian reputation, the militia inevitably clashed with the local authorities.[50]

IV

How accurate were the allegations of a mean and schismatic militia? Obviously further research is needed, but it is clear that there was regional variation. Somerset, where the radical John Pyne faction controlled the militia, conforms to the stereotype.[51] Cheshire and Berkshire, it would appear, were the same.[52] Yet in Sussex control was placed firmly in the hands of the conservative gentry.[53] As far as the nation as a whole is concerned, we do know that Baptists and Fifth Monarchists got commissions.[54] So did the hated Quakers: former officers and justices, merchants and shopkeepers. Nicholas Bond, William Woodcock, Amos Stoddart, Richard Davis, and Steven Hart, were named commissioners for the Westminster militia in late June.[55] In July other Quakers appeared in the lists for the counties: George Lambol and Thomas Curtis were named for Berkshire, Edward Alcock for Cheshire, Humphrey Lower for Cornwall, Henry Pollexfen for Devon, Mark Grime for Gloucestershire, John Gawler for Glamorganshire, Theophilus Alie for Worcestershire, and Edward Stoakes for Wiltshire. The Robert Duncon named as a Suffolk commissioner may have been the Quaker Robert Duncon. The Michael Munckton on the Lincolnshire list was a Quaker at the Restoration, but we are not sure of his sympathies in 1659.[56] In Bristol Thomas Speed, Dennis Hollister, Henry Rowe, Thomas Gouldney, and Edward Pyott, all well-known Quakers, served as commissioners. Vane had pressed unsuccessfully for George Bishop's inclusion.[57] Finally, in north-west Wales Quakers were represented by Robert Owen, Owen Lewis, Owen Humphreys, Thomas Ellis, Richard Jones, and probably Charles Lloyd, a sympathizer who later became a Quaker.[58]

Other Quakers served in the militia later in the year. We know that Anthony Pearson raised forces in the North at the time of the Booth rebellion because he got into trouble for it after the Restoration. Thomas Ellwood may have been an ensign in the Oxford militia. Peter Acklam, the commander of a militia troop at Hull, was a Quaker by the early 1660s, but it is uncertain when he became one. Mark Jellico, one of those responsible for raising men in Cheshire after the downfall of the Rump, may well have been the Chester Quaker mentioned in *Mercurius Publicus* in 1661 and into his fifth offence under the Conventicle Act by 1670. And there was Captain Carter, at large in Cheshire in February

1660 with the armed troop of horse he had raised under the Committee of Safety. The authorities claimed he was a Quaker; the Quakers grudgingly admitted it though they made it clear that they no longer owned him.[59]

If Quaker pleas for reinstatement in the forces are any indication, it must be assumed that they were among those who flocked to the various volunteer regiments raised at the time of the Booth rising. Quaker sources are strangely silent, apart from Fox's later comments about 'foolish rash spirits' and a reference to Quakers in trouble in the early 1660s for their role in the suppression of Booth.[60] But it is hard to believe that there would have been no Quaker volunteers in Colonel John Haggatt's Bristol regiment, or among Vane's Southwark volunteers, Colonel William West's forces in Lancashire, John Bradshaw's Cheshire volunteers, or the Northamptonshire militia under the command of William Rainborough.[61] Nor is it unreasonable to assume that John Pyne, in charge of the foot in Somerset, would have made use of his old Quaker associates from county committee days: Robert Wastfield, James Pearce, Jasper Batt, Christopher Pittard, and John Anderdon – all had declared their readiness to serve the Commonwealth.[62] Colonel Bussy Mansell, whom the Rump placed in command of all militia forces in south Wales, was eager to have Quakers in his regiments; and he had many Quaker ex-officers to draw from. A few engaged: a captain and a lieutenant-colonel. Others wanted Fox's advice. Fox claimed he 'for bad' it. But that was after the event. We do not know what advice he gave his Welsh friends at the time.[63]

It is harder to substantiate rumours of a sectarian-dominated Army, although it is easy to see why conservatives would have been concerned. Fifth Monarchists certainly gained commands with the accession of the Rump, as did Baptists.[64] Quaker sources are silent apart from later claims that Quakers refused commissions offered by the Committee of Safety.[65] Many Quakers (minor officers and rank and file) who had been purged from the Army earlier for their beliefs, insubordination, or because they had refused the oath of fidelity to the Protectorate, were calling for reinstatement. But if the Quakers were willing, what of the Rump and Army?

Most of the evidence is hazy. John Lambert's regiment, we shall see later, was thought to be rife with Quakerism. Nathaniel Rich had Quakers in his forces, though it is not clear whether he

was encouraging them or trying to get rid of them.[66] Robert
Lilburne's own cornet, George Denham, was either a Quaker or
a sympathizer; and Lilburne himself may have died a Quaker.
Lilburne's regiment had been purged of Quakers by Monck in
1657, so it is possible that they were readmitted in the heady days
of the recalled Rump.[67] It would be surprising if no Quakers were
restored to Richard Ashfield's forces. His regiment had also been
cleansed of Quakerism by Monck in 1657. Ashfield was probably
not a Quaker (Fox claimed he was), but he was certainly
sympathetic and retained contacts with Quakers throughout
1659.[68]

The Quaker John Hodgson re-enlisted.[69] The forces stationed
at Manchester in October had Quakers among them.[70] Robert
Owen, the Rump's commander at Beaumaris in Anglesey, was a
Quaker by early 1660, but we do not know whether this was the
case in 1659. The governor of the garrison at Cardiff, Colonel
Mark Grime, was probably the same man as the Gloucestershire
Quaker Colonel Mark Grime.[71] With the regiment of James
Berry we are on safer ground. During the reorganization of the
Army in May, Berry nominated the Quakers Edward Billing and
Richard Ward as cornets in his regiment, Ward in Berry's own
troop. They were approved by Parliament. His captain, Thomas
Wells, was also a Quaker. Billing was well known, so his
appointment would not have gone unnoticed. (Billing and Ward
had been purged from Berry's forces by Monck.) Billing later
reported that a divided Rump had concluded, after much debate,
that he should have a command if he took the oath of abjuration,
but it seems that he refused to comply with the terms of the
commission.[72] Others were less fortunate. The William
Tomlinson who claimed that he had been dismissed on
ideological grounds and who tried unsuccessfully for readmission
to the Army was probably William Tomlinson the Quaker.[73]

Quaker preachers were active in the Army throughout 1659.
Burrough and Samuel Fisher went to Dunkirk in May, holding
meetings of 'some hundreds of officers and souilders'. The two
Quakers claimed that they were a success: 'a great love Raised in
ye souilders towards us'. And they reported fears that 'ye hole
armie should bee seduced to follow us'.[74] In Manchester, in
September, Hubberthorne held great meetings in the town hall,
gatherings which were attended by soldiers (officers had given
him the keys to the hall).[75] Quaker ministers held meetings

among the soldiers in Scotland despite rumours that Monck was about to move against them. But they had little success, except with 'some few officers who did decline from Monke'.[76]

v

The year witnessed steadily increasing hostility towards the Quakers, a hostility tinged with both fear and hatred. That the gentry and ministry should loathe the Quakers was to be expected. Quaker disrespect for social gradations was notorious, their doctrine was subversive, they were out to overthrow the ministry and disturb the peace. Popular hostility was a different matter, a mixture, I have argued in chapter 4, of xenophobia, class hatred and superstition. But it was shaped and stimulated by indoctrinating anti-Quaker propaganda. The lesson of 1659 is that we should not underestimate the effects of pamphlet and sermon. Hostility was instilled through the pulpit. The rapid increase in Quaker numbers was astounding. Their relentless campaign against the state church by harassment of ministers and opposition to tithes, their persistent petitioning, gave the ministry a feeling that it was threatened, that it was under siege. As a New England opponent said of the sect, probably in 1658, 'There is more danger in this people to trouble and overcome England, then the King of Scots, and all the Popish Princes in Germany'.[77]

Though they felt isolated, ministers were not short of suggestions as to how to deal with the Quaker menace. 'Magistrates should not bee as Jupiters log, which by lying still, and doing nothing, made the frogs bold with it', Ralph Farmer told the magistrates of Bristol.[78] If justices were generally ahead of governments in their severity towards Quakers, ministers, particularly Presbyterians, were ahead of the magistrates. A Lancashire minister complained to a Quaker in 1659 that the magistrates were 'Faulty in that they did not sheath their swords in the Bowells of such Blasphemers as you are'. Another, this time in Bath, shortly before the Booth rising, wanted 'three or four Quakers hanged for an example'. If Saint Paul had been alive he would have stoned Quakers; 'it was Christian zeal to stone them'; 'if the Lawes were right, they would chop off all the Quakers heads'.[79]

The Cornish priest who said that he would carry 'a Pistoll in his pockett, and a sword by his side to defend himselfe from ye

Quakers', captured perfectly the phobia which formed the background to the Royalist-Presbyterian risings planned for 1659.[80] 'Do not the same Priests now . . . stir up the people against us they then called Round-heads, and now called Quakers?' asked the Quaker Humphrey Smith in a tract in 1658.[81] The Quakers claimed that the pulpit could 'Poyson a whole Nation, and leaven them with malice, against whom they please'; 1659 confirmed them in this belief.[82] They were sensitive to the growing panic, and reported hostile sermons. John Hodder, a minister in Dorset, had said in 1658 that 'if his Lord Protector would raise an Army to cutt off all the Quakers, he would be the first man that would draw the sword'. In 1659 a Cornish minister, 'haveing chosen these words for his Text follow peace with all Men', explained to his congregation 'they were not to follow peace with sectaryes'.[83] Fox claimed that it was being preached that 'Quakers would kill', 'the Quakers would rise'.[84]

Bishop, the Bristol Quaker, was said to have written 'it would never bee well' 'until [Edmund] Calamy, and some other of the Priests were dealt withal as [Christopher] Love was' – in other words, executed.[85] Rumours abounded in the months before the Booth rebellion. A Sussex Quaker had called out to a priest, 'We will have you all down, for now our day is come'; another, that 'he no more cared to kill one of the Priests, then he would to kill a Dog'. It was reported that a Sussex minister had been waylaid by a Quaker with a drawn sword. In Kent a colleague testified that he heard Luke Howard, a leading Kentish Quaker, claim a revelation in July 'that the priests shall be destroyed, and by the people who are called Quakers'.[86]

In July Robert South was preparing the congregation at St Mary's, Oxford, for 'the worst that can happen. Should God in his judgment suffer England to be transformed into a Münster'.[87] William Prynne had expressed similar apprehensions two months earlier.[88] It was probably about this time that Quakers were alleged to have burnt houses in Oxford, and to have threatened to do the same in Middlesex.[89] Occasionally the undercurrent of uncertainty revealed itself in more concrete terms. The Devonshire town of Tiverton awakened at midnight on 14 July to the cry that Quakers, Fifth Monarchists, and Anabaptists had combined 'not only to cut the Throats of the Godly in that Town, but the throats of all the Godly in the Nation that Night'.[90]

Past indiscretions were conjured up to blacken the sect and whip up anti-Quaker feeling. People were reminded of the excesses of James Nayler, John Toldervy, and John Gilpin, of Christopher Atkinson's 'frequent fornication' with another leading Quaker's maid. There were new charges of immorality, of incest, buggery, and witchcraft. Some Quakers, it was said, 'had killed their Mother, following the light within them'. The often bizarre behaviour of the sect added grist to the mill. Solomon Eccles's interruption of the prominent minister Edmund Calamy in early July, when the Quaker climbed into the pulpit and began sewing, was publicized to good effect. A Norwich man lay trouserless and trembling on a communion table; another burst into Aldermanbury Church with arms and hands 'all besmeared with Excrements'.[91]

Quakers were attacked during the months before August. A meeting in Vine Street in London was set upon by mobs in June and July. Other attacks occurred in parts of Lancashire and Cheshire. Quakers clashed with the inhabitants of Brentford (in Middlesex), though details are obscure.[92] It is often impossible to determine the exact motives for hostility. Episodes sometimes look more like robberies or sexual attacks, but occasionally they betrayed an underlying hatred. In Somerset in July a woman was set upon and forced to swear 'by the Lord's Blood' that she was not a Quaker.[93] Some episodes were comical. A meeting held some time in 1659 was broken up by an imaginative Kentish churchwarden who tossed a dead cat, fish, and magpie into the crowd of Quakers and then unleashed his hounds.[94] Others were more serious. In Sawbridgeworth in Hertfordshire, the scene of later trouble at the time of the Booth rising, a Quaker meeting was attacked in early July. The Quakers alleged that the mob had been encouraged by justices, that when they had approached Sir Thomas Hewet for protection he bid them 'go for remedy to them that gave them their Liberty'.[95] Similar claims were made in Liskeard in Cornwall. Here Quakers were set upon by a crowd stirred up by a minister – 'some of the Rabble were Men of Figure, and one a Magistrate of the Town'.[96]

VI

The most impressive demonstration of the Quaker fear came with the series of attempted Royalist-Presbyterian risings at the end of July when generalized fear of Quakerism was fanned by more specific, clearly induced, rumours of impending sectarian risings and Quaker plots. Royalists were aware of this feeling. Indeed the Viscount Mordaunt's correspondence betrays hints of a forthcoming defensive reaction. 'The Quakers appear in great bodies in several places, and it alarms us', he wrote to Clarendon in June; (and again to Charles) 'in a few days we shall order it so as we hope we may be able to defend ourselves against the storm of Quakers and Anabaptists'.[97]

The only momentarily successful insurrection was that led by Sir George Booth in Cheshire and south Lancashire. Booth's 'Letter to a Friend', generally taken as reflecting his true aims, made it clear that one of the issues of the rising was the feeling that both religion and the gentry's traditional position were being threatened: 'by raising among us a Militia, they cut off our right Hand, by subjecting us under the meanest and most fanatick Spirits of the Nation'.[98] This was how others greeted the rising. 'They would perswade the poor ignorant people that their Gospel is lost, and their God lost, and all gone, if this Parliament be not broken', reported the *Publick Intelligencer* at the beginning of August. Henry Stubbe said, in October, that the main issue of Booth's rising 'was Toleration, or no Toleration, rather than Monarchy and the Stuartian interest'. According to him, the rebellion had been against the sects. The Quaker Francis Howgil thought the same. The ministers had 'preached up the people into Rebellion upon pain of Damnation'; 'and all this quarrel they said, was against the Quakers'.[99]

Many ministers do seem to have played an important part in the rising. If they did not actually incite people on the eve of the rebellion, then at least they helped by encouraging the state of mind which made it possible. Mr Stockport of Manchester invited the 'people to arms upon the score of the Quakers being up'. In Cheadle, the day before the insurrection, the minister endeavoured 'to stir up the pishoners there to betake themselves to Armes. As that they should stand upp and be valiant for the Defence of theire libertye for (sd hee) the Quakers were now upp, & the Neck of Religion lay uppon the block'. Adam Martindale, a Presbyterian minister, claimed that much of Booth's support was enrolled 'under pretence of danger from the Quakers'. This happened in Manchester, Warrington, Cheadle, and Chester. And in Bolton and Bury ministers preached 'yt Religion was in dainger, and yt whatsoever was undertaken was onely agst

Quakers and those who would destroy ye Ministry, and moving and exhorting ale men for to take up armes as for Gods own cause, and used that Text of Scripture Curse yee Merosh & c'.[100]

Outside Cheshire and Lancashire the projected risings were dismal failures. But fear of the Quakers was widespread. In Oxford, at the end of July, noises on the roof and a bugle blast convinced the occupants of Carfax Church that 'the day of judgment was at hand', that 'anabaptists and quakers were come to cut their throats'.[101] Devon and Somerset experienced some alarm. Apart from the Tiverton episode (described earlier), there were allegations that a Quaker had killed a minister; while newsbooks reported fears in July and early August that 'Anabaptists and Quakers were joyned together to cut the Throats of all the Ministers and Magistrates in those parts'.[102] In Cambridge anti-Quaker feeling was whipped up, probably intentionally, for the incident in question had happened several years before, by allegations of witchcraft.[103] In Sawbridgeworth in Hertfordshire a mob attacked a Quaker meeting; Quakers were beaten and a house destroyed. The Quakers claimed connivance by certain justices, and warned Parliament: 'This last Tragedy was acted the immediate day before the intended insurrection, and the Actors expressed great confidence of the success thereof, saying, That there is no Parliament, and that King Charles would not allow such meetings'.[104]

A vague report in *Mercurius Politicus* seems to imply that Derbyshire and Leicestershire ministers had used fears of impending massacre at the hands of sectaries to mobilize support for the planned risings.[105] In Wiltshire there were rumours that 'many Quakers' were 'up'.[106] Men were engaged in Hampshire and in Salop to 'go and fight against the Quakers'.[107] In Gloucestershire, too, a minister was recruiting men for the rising, persuading them that 'the Anabaptists and Quakers would pull downe the light of the gospell & the ministry if a course were not taken with them'.[108] When Nicholas Rookewood Esquire of Kirby in Norfolk was asked to account for his private armoury, he said it was 'to secure himselfe agaynst Quakers & Annibaptists who he feared would ryse to Cutt his throat, & if they did soe he was resolved to cutt theire throats First if he could'.[109]

VII

Rumours and accusations were still flying after the Booth

debacle. Philip Henry, a minister from Worthenbury in Flintshire, noted that Lambert's forces who suppressed the rising espoused 'the Quakers' cause' and offered 'injury to some ministers'. Their victory seemed somehow symbolized by the trooper sitting hatted in Henry's church during the singing of psalms.[110]

Anti-Quaker propaganda was still rife. There was talk in September of a coven of Anabaptist and Quaker witches in Sherborne in Dorset.[111] Lord Saye and Sele recalled that Felton, the murderer of the Duke of Buckingham, had said that he 'had impulses of the spirit moving him to do so'; and the lord repeated a story that a Quaker in the North, 'met riding with a cord about his middle', had said that the spirit had sent him to hang a minister.[112] Richard Blome wrote in November of 'talk by some Quakers of dividing mens estates and having all things common'. Saye and Sele agreed: 'the truth is, under the shew and vizard of religion, you carry on a Levelling principle'.[113] And there was the inevitable comparison between the Quakers and the Münster Anabaptists.[114]

At the beginning of October, a Quaker shop in Tower Street in London was set upon when it opened on a Sunday.[115] Ugly situations developed in Newark-on-Trent in November and again in December when Quakers were attacked by a mob armed with staffs, knives, and what appears to have been the seventeenth-century version of a Molotov cocktail. Again Quakers charged the JPs with complacency.[116]

The French ambassador, Bordeaux, realized as early as June that 'dread of the Sectaries' was a crucial factor in the increasing desire for the restoration of Charles Stuart.[117] By September the desire was stronger. This 'infinite liberty' and time of 'hideous errors', a time when some 'would have turned things up-side down', was how Edward Reynolds, the future Bishop of Norwich, described it on 5 November to the Mayor and aldermen of London. 'Certainly since the reformation of Religion the Ministers of the Gospel have never been under more reproach and contempt', he told them again in December.[118] God was abandoning England. Popery was returning 'under the disguise of Sectaries', 'especially Quakers'. There was speculation of a 'second Deluge of Antichristianisme over the Protestant Churches'.[119]

Some called for unity to combat heresy and division.

Independents joined Presbyterians in their 'utter dislike and abhorrence of a Universal Toleration'. The two had been moving closer in several areas to meet the threat of Quakers and other sectaries: in Cheshire, Newcastle, and Somerset, for instance.[120] They met with Baptists in London in September and October 'for reconciliation and cooperation for ordinances against Quakers', resulting, it seems, in a declaration in favour of tithes and against universal toleration. This paper, presented to the Committee of Safety, also demanded that 'countenance be not given unto nor trust reposed in the hands of Quakers'.[121]

'The short of [it] all is . . . the Nation is certainly destroyed', a pamphlet had claimed in August, 'and no person in the World, besides the King, is in a capacity to avert the impendent ruin'.[122] Many were beginning to agree. William Callow, a Manx Quaker, was told that the King 'would ridd the Land of Quakers'. 'Who ever heard of Ranters, Quakers, &c under the King?' someone asked Baxter.[123] In September William Prynne had been calling for the restoration of the monarchy; in November Alice Thornton was praying for it; by the beginning of 1660, according to Lucy Hutchinson, the Presbyterians were preaching for it 'and began openly to desire the king; not for good will to him, but only for destruction to all the fanatics'.[124]

The Quaker fear had yet another role to play. Monck's march south, which made the Restoration possible, was a move against sectarianism. Preservation of religion and the ministry was his 'grand motive', the General claimed after his declaration for the Rump in October. In February of the following year he explained his support in Scotland: 'nothing was more dreadful to them, then a fear to be over-run with Phanatique Notions'. Monck's chaplain John Price told him 'that if things did continue in this State much longer, it would be found that the Quaker would be as great a Goad in the sides of our new Sects, as ever the Old Puritan was to the Church of England'.[125]

An old enemy to Quakerism, George Monck became fully identified with the anti-sectarian cause. He purged his army of sectaries, and it became the only hope against a sectarian dominated English Army and the Anabaptists' 'design to set up themselves alone'. The forces of Monck's opponent, John Lambert, were said to contain Quakers who 'bargained for, and sold Horses, to be paid when such or such a Steeple-House . . . was pulled down'.[126] Monck entered London as a saviour of

religion, 'England's St. George'.[127] His remodelled army quickly
established itself as the scourge of the Quakers, 'beinge as they
said bound in an oath to Leive never a sectarian in England'.[128]
'He took Rebellion rampant, by the Throat, And made the
Canting Quaker change his Note.'[129]

The General's task had been made easier by Thomas, Lord
Fairfax's actions in York at the end of December.[130] Here too the
rising was of a conservative, Presbyterian nature. The Royalist Sir
Philip Monckton claimed that a Quaker fear, not unlike that
during the Booth rebellion, eventually persuaded many wavering
gentry to support Fairfax; and his claims seem to have had some
basis. There were rumours of Quakers arming and combining to
support Lambert in a bid for liberty of conscience, talk of a
Quaker rendezvous at Lilburne's house near York. Again
military action assumed a defensive guise. The gentry had risen, it
was reported, to prevent an unholy alliance between Lambert and
the Quakers.[131]

An earlier coup in Ireland also reflected the ascendancy of
Presbyterian interests. On 13 December Sir Theophilus Jones, Sir
Charles Coote, Lord Broghill and others seized power,
professedly on behalf of the Rump. Their declaration betrayed
their real concerns. The coup was aimed at Baptists and Quakers
– 'unclean Spirits' – in an attempt to arrest what the gentry saw as
the rapid slide into 'Münster Desolations', a repetition of the
'German Tragedy'. Regiments were purged. The newly formed
forces, it was said, boasted that their principal battle was with the
Quakers.[132]

Throughout January and February 1660 the gentry and
ministers agitated for readmission of the secluded members to the
re-restored Rump. What some of them expected of their
Parliament was obvious from their petitions pressing for its
recall: suppression of the sects.[133] When the secluded members
took their places in Parliament on 21 February the Restoration
was inevitable. Reaction was firmly entrenched by the time
Charles crossed the Channel to England. History was already
being rewritten. Quakers, Baptists, the Rump, the Army, were
already mixed under the soubriquet 'fanatic'. The Quakers were
firmly identified with the radicalism and excesses of 1659.[134]

Rumours and fears of Quakers in arms did not vanish; indeed
they became part of the political make-up of the early 1660s. It
was alleged at the end of February that the commanders of the

garrison at Shrewsbury had planned, with the help of Quakers and Baptists, to seize the castle against Parliament.[135] Feelings that sectaries, discontented Rumpers, and the Army would combine against the secluded members (and the Convention Parliament after them) came to a head in April with John Lambert's escape from the Tower. Samuel Pepys captured the seriousness of the situation: 'it is now clear that either the Fanatiques must now be undone, or the Gentry and citizens throughout England and clergy must fall'. Lambert was thought to have the support of Baptists and Quakers as well as that of disbanded soldiers. It was even said that Quakers were selling estates to raise money for the cause.[136] In the end, however, he alienated many radicals – certainly the Quakers – by declaring for Richard Cromwell. His disorganized followers were easily routed.[137]

The gentry were meanwhile on the offensive. The secluded members put power firmly into their hands in March with the Militia Act: in Cheshire nearly all those named as commissioners had been Booth supporters.[138] Sectaries could expect little sympathy from such men or from a Parliament which was busily dividing the nation into Presbyterian classes. Local solutions had been made well before the King landed.

In York, from January onwards, Quaker meetings were broken up by order of the Mayor and aldermen and the meeting-house doors were nailed up. During the following months the authorities pursued a policy of harassment. Troops were posted to prevent Quakers from gathering, and watches in April and early May – a method also used in Norwich[139] – attempted to stop Quakers entering the city.[140] Elsewhere the pattern was probably much the same. Quakers seem to have been purged from the Navy.[141] Meetings were broken up in Wales and London.[142] The Irish Council talked at the end of February of banishing all sectaries; Quakers reported that in Ireland during the early months of 1660 their meetings were smashed, that in some towns Quakers were banned altogether.[143] There were mob attacks – in Bristol, in Glastonbury (Somerset), in Plymouth. May witnessed many violent attacks on Quakers in Cambridge, Devon, and Dorset. In Essex a mob combined with some sailors to attack Quakers in Harwich, with cries of 'the King is now coming, who will hang or banish you all'.[144]

VIII

And so the King came back at the end of May 1660 on the crest of a wave of reaction against the 'immense and boundless liberty' of 1659. His restoration became enshrined as an act of divine intervention. Religion had been rescued from subversion at the hands of the sects by a 'wonderful whirlwind', Baxter reminded the Mayor, aldermen and companies of London in a thanksgiving sermon.[145] The Protestant religion, wrote George Willington of Bristol, had 'been in great danger of being rooted out by Anabaptists, Quakers, and Atheists'.[146] A learned ministry had been 'reproached, ready to be sacrificed, brought to the brow of the precipice'. There had been fears of a return to popery. But Charles, defender of the faith, had returned to quell divisions. 'Have not Coblers, Draymen, Mechanics Governed, as well as preached?', Robert South, future chaplain to the Earl of Clarendon, asked his presumably sympathetic audience at Lincoln's Inn. 'Nay have not they by Preaching come to Govern? Was ever that of Solomon more verified, that Servants have Rid, while Princes, and Nobles have gone on Foot.'[147] But now, exclaimed William Brownsword, the Presbyterian vicar of Kendal, in a sermon welcoming his King, 'God is blasting our Phanatick enemies; and we are in a way to Religious as well as Civil settlement'.[148]

The events of 1659 may be compared with the fear of Catholic plots in England in the early 1640s or the Great Fear in France over a century later.[149] It was *Grande Peur* and fear of Catholics in reverse, however. The generalized suspicion and terror encouraged by pulpit and print stimulated reaction, not revolution. As Georges Lefebvre found of the rural panic of 1789, myth swamped reality. What became important was not what was happening but what people thought was happening. Yet (to draw on the French parallel again) fear, in turn, shaped events. 1659's legacy to the nation was Charles Stuart and the paranoia of the early Restoration period. For the Quakers the year yielded equal disaster. As Alexander Parker wrote to George Fox in August 1660, 'better had it been if all had been kept still & Quiet in those times, for because of ye forwardnesse, and want of wisedome in some is one great cause of our prsent sufferings'.[150]

PART IV　EPILOGUE

CHAPTER 6

The transformation of Quakerism

I

Josiah Langdale was born in 1673 in Nafferton, in Yorkshire. He attended school as a child, and when his father died returned home to help his mother on their farm. By the age of ten he was keeping cows and ploughing. His family were not Quakers, though Josiah (as he later recalls) was 'religiously inclined'. Husbandry did not leave time for formal schooling, but Langdale could read the Bible and had learned some Latin. He was soon an expert with the plough, and at the tender age of thirteen could 'go with Four horses, & plow alone. . . . I very much delighted in holding the Plow, It being an Employment Sutable to my Mind, & no Company to disturb my Contemplation'.[1]

When Josiah was sixteen his mother remarried and the youth became a servant in husbandry, hiring himself out by the year. His second employer was a Quaker. Thus began Langdale's slow introduction to Quakerism. His religious education continued. He befriended a workmate, a blind thresher who could memorize sermons and large passages of Scripture. The two would 'walk out' together 'on First-Day [Sunday] Mornings in the Summer time several Miles a-foot, to hear such Priests as were the most famed for Preaching; and as we walked together we should have such Talk as was profitable'. They would sit in a field with a Bible: 'and after I have read a while we have sat silent, waiting with Desires in our Hearts after the Lord; and as we thus sate waiting and weeping, the Lord did often comfort us'.[2]

Langdale renewed his contract with his Quaker master, and became a foreman. He was happy with his employers, his 'master and dame'. They did not press their beliefs upon him; indeed he was still totally ignorant of Quaker theology. Yet he was attracted by the demeanour of the Quakers whom he encountered in the day-to-day activity of the fair and market place, by 'their grave Carriage and sober Behaviour, with

Fewness of Words that they used in Dealing & Trading'. He began to feel uncomfortable whenever he returned home to visit family and friends, thinking them 'vain wanton and full of Frothiness'.[3] Eventually it was suggested that he attend a Quaker meeting, and, gradually, Josiah was converted. By 1693, at the age of twenty, he was a Quaker. He attended meetings, dispensed with the niceties of social etiquette, and rejected flattering titles. On Sundays, he would be up before sunrise, tramping across the fields to the nearest meeting house. He would go without food for the whole day; attending his first meeting from 11 a.m. to 3 p.m., sitting under a hedge until the second gathering at 5 p.m., and in the evening, when it had finished, walking home across the fields.[4]

This picture is in marked contrast to the ecstatic goings on some forty years earlier in Malton, a mere twenty miles over the Wolds.[5] There is no eager proselytizing; for several years Langdale's Quaker employers had not even broached the subject of religion. Meetings were not the enthusiastic, tub-thumping gatherings of earlier years. Some 'at Times wept', occasionally someone would speak, but meetings were usually silent affairs, sometimes for hours on end. Friends 'appeared solid & grave, & sat with Reverence upon their Minds, like a People worshipping God in Spirit'.[6] Nor is there much evidence of riven families or local turmoil. At first, Josiah's mother was 'greatly displeased' by his unusual carriage; 'She said I was bewitched, & that she would never own me to be her Son more'. Her displeasure did not last for long. In fact his relatives were tolerant. An aunt recalled the early days of the Quaker movement; she claimed that they were not now so resolute in their testimony against extravagances in dress.[7]

Langdale's experiences mirror the changes in the Quaker movement after 1660. 1660 is the crucial year in Quaker history, the commencement of what has been accurately termed the 'second period' of Quakerism. The Restoration began with a fight for survival, for the Quakers (along with purchasers of Crown lands, Commonwealthsmen, Fifth Monarchists, and one-time members of the New Model Army) were labelled implacable opponents of the monarchy.[8] Energies which had formerly been engaged in conflict with the world were channelled into forming a haven within it. The Quakers strove to create their own world, an alternative community. This change was gradual; never total; and it built on tendencies that were already evident in the 1650s. But between 1660 and 1700 the Quaker movement was transformed, ideologically, organizationally, culturally.

II

The Restoration began badly for Friends. When the King returned in 1660 there were rumours that Charles was about to banish the sect, 'or hang us all'.[9] They were, it was said of the Bristol branch of the sect, irreconcilable enemies of the monarchy: 'psons of very dangerous principalls, & evil Enimies . . . to his Maties royall pson, Govment, & restauration, & some of them, petitioners to bringe His Martired Matie of blessed Memory to His Triall'.[10] Long before specific legislation was enacted against the Quakers in the form of the Quaker Act of 1662, justices and local militias were harassing and detaining members of the sect, and raiding meetings. The authorities in most counties moved against the Quakers. Dorset justices organized raids on meetings in Hawkchurch, Sherborne, Cerne Abbas, Blandford, Weymouth, and Poole.[11] In Berkshire at the end of May (the month of the King's restoration) the militia broke up the Kingston Lisle meeting with some violence; when asked for their warrant 'one of them held his sword at the freind that asked and said that was his warrant'.[12] Several Quakers were wounded in the same month when their Cambridge meeting was attacked by soldiers.[13] The Governor of Portsmouth sent his troops to deal with the sect; individuals were detained, meetings dispersed, recalcitrants from outside Portsmouth thrown out of town.[14] In separate incidents in Gloucestershire, militiamen threatened to hang – to the extent of putting the rope round the victim's neck – and shoot Quakers while searching their houses for arms.[15] Arrests were frequently selective. In Sussex Sir Humphrey Bennet secured 'the head and cheife' of 'anabaptists and quakers'. George Fox the younger and Robert Grassingham, both leading Quakers, were arrested in Essex, joining potential troublemakers (prominent Army officers and Fifth Monarchists) under the custody of the Serjeant-at-arms.[16] The Cheshire authorities seized another important Quaker, Alexander Parker; and George Fox was detained in Lancaster from June until October as 'an Enemy to our sovereign Lord the King and a chief upholder of the Quakers sect'.[17]

In January 1661, in the wake of an abortive Fifth Monarchist rising, Quakers throughout the country were taken out of meetings, out of their homes, from their places of work, and from off the streets: by March nearly five thousand Friends were in prison.[18] The gentry had shown little reluctance to restore what they saw as 'the good society'. 'If . . . the King would authorize me to do it', an Oxfordshire deputy-lieutenant told Thomas Ellwood, 'I would not leave a Quaker alive in England, Except you. I would make no more . . . to set my Pistol to their Ears, and shoot them through the Head, than I would to kill a Dog.' When Edward Billing was set upon by a mob after he had attempted to disrupt the consecration of the Archbishop of Canterbury, a 'greate one formerly called a Cavaleere sayd trouble not a Magistrate with him dash out his braines. Marke they are like dogs in time of plague they are to be killed as they go up and downe ye streetes yt they do not infect.'[19]

The Quaker Act of 1662 and the better-known Conventicle Act of 1664 provided for fining, imprisonment, and transportation of Quakers taken at meetings. But these were not the only weapons used against the sect. Old Elizabethan and Jacobean statutes, intended originally for use against popish recusants, were revived to deal with the movement. The authorities had an impressive arsenal to use against the Quakers, though for various reasons, too detailed to go into here, the gentry did not make full use of their armoury.[20] Still, no one can doubt that the Quakers were under a state of siege during the Restoration period. Persecution tended to come in waves: in the aftermath of the passing of the Quaker Act, after the Northern Plot of 1663, in the wake of the passage of the first and second Conventicle Acts of 1664 and 1670, at the end of the 1670s after Charles II ordered the enforcement of the penal laws, and in the early 1680s when the sect was victimized because of its support of the Whigs. A survey of Quaker sufferings 1660-80, which was released in 1680, claimed a total number of Quaker imprisonments of nearly 11,000, and 243 deaths, presumably mostly in prison – and these figures do not include fines and a miscellany of harassments.[21]

III

One often reads of Quaker quietism during the Restoration period. The Quakers, as Alan Cole has put it, retreated into their tents after 1660. They despaired of righteous government ever being established by human agency; had not man failed and failed again? And so they reasoned that history demonstrated that providence worked by a kind of 'divine empiricism': successive regimes had been tried and, found wanting, dashed one against the other – 'pot-sherds of the earth'.[22] The notion of Quaker withdrawal is a valid one. Some Friends sought solace in apocalyptic ranting. 'I am comeing in Ten Thousands of my saints, yea in thousands of thousands of those poore people wch have been long as trodden downe', God told William Bayly; 'fear not their kings nor their Princes, their Parliaments, nor their Rulers, for I will Trample upon kings, & Princes as upon Morters in this ye day of my fury.'[23] John Hill, in 1661, predicted a day of terrible persecution followed by an earthquake which would shake open the prison doors and free all the saints; 'shortly after yt time great destruction shall come upon ye wicked'.[24] But for most, political defeat reinforced faith in the need for a longer-term, spiritual regeneration of humankind before the millennium could be realized. The cause of liberty, it seemed, would not be advanced by militant, political means.

Thus we get the first clear declarations of Quaker pacifism. We 'are now better informed than once we were', Edward Burrough told the King in May 1660, 'for though we do now more than ever oppose Oppression, and seek after Reformation, yet we do it not in that way of outward Warring & Fighting with Carnal Weapons, & Swords.'[25] He 'that hath commandeth us, That we shall not swear at all, Mat. 5.34', George Fox, Richard Hubberthorne, and others declared in early 1661, 'hath also Commanded us, That we shall not kill'. 'And all Plots, Insurrections, and Riotous Meetings, we do deny'.[26]

Yet one should not exaggerate the *political passivity* of Restoration Quakerism. Not all Quakers withdrew into their tents, and those who did still ventured forth from time to time. Indeed as F.B. Tolles has pointed out, there really is no such thing as *a* Quaker attitude to politics.[27] Events in the North American colonies in the latter half of the seventeenth century may demonstrate a degree of practical inexperience on the part of Friends in affairs of state, but they by no means indicate any political reticence. Quakers served as governors, deputy governors, and assemblymen in Maryland, Rhode Island, Pennsylvania, West New Jersey, and the Carolinas. They also held a variety of other offices: that of provincial commissioner, justice of the peace, and town selectman.[28] As the English

Quakers of the 1650s had proclaimed, if the situation was propitious they were willing and able to serve. In Restoration England, of course, the times never seemed right, but Quakers there were certainly not apolitical. They pressed the case for religious toleration, and were thus for a while aligned with the Whigs. By the late 1670s central Quaker organization was liaising with meetings in the counties to mobilize Quaker support for suitable non-Quaker parliamentary candidates. The Quakers were by then an acknowledged, formidable lobbying group, able to bring pressure in Court and Parliament.[29]

It is also becoming clear that the famous Quaker peace testimony was slower in developing and less universally accepted after 1660 than most historians have assumed. When the Quaker Thomas Laycock appeared before the Ely Assizes in 1660 for seditious words, it was for saying, in Wisbech market place, 'that he did never beare arms but if ever he did it should be against Charles Stuart'.[30] 'As if in a Civil State or Common-wealth there were no use or place for such things', Robert Rich replied to Fox's criticism of fellow Quaker John Perrot for wearing a sword; 'what is more meet and proper to obtain and keep and defend carnal things than carnal weapons?'[31] It was doubtful that God intended to use 'that way of warring wth carnall weapons', an unknown Quaker wrote in April 1660 at the time of John Lambert's rising, 'for in our dayes the Lord semes not by yt way to appeare, as formerly but by another secrett hand'. Yet the Quaker did not entirely rule out the use of force. Warfare could be legitimate if the individual concerned felt 'in his owne conscience by ye devine principle' that 'he was called of god thereunto'.[32] The Yorkshire Quaker who said that 'if God put ye sword into his hands he must strike' seems to have been thinking along such lines.[33] Two Norfolk Quakers were in trouble in 1662 for threatening that if the Quaker Act was enforced 'rather than wee will be undone by Fynes or sent away at the kings pleasure we will fight for it'.[34] Pacifism came slowly for the Kentish merchant seaman Edward Coxere: 'I did not lay down fighting on other men's words, but the Lord taught me to love my enemies in his own time.' Coxere claimed that some Quaker seamen either rejected the sect's stand on warfare or were deceitful about it.[35]

I emphasize this lack of commitment to pacifism not because it was widespread – as far as we know it was not – but because it is seldom mentioned in histories of Restoration Quakerism. Edward Billing twice refused to declare himself a 'loyal subject', or even to promise not to plot against the King.[36] John Pennyman claimed in 1691 that there had been earlier dissension over the peace testimony; and the famous peace declaration of 1661 does lack some important Quaker signatures.[37] One missing name was that of George Fox the younger, who had written to the monarch in 1660: 'it had been better for thee that thou hadst never come', and who was to be under threat of arrest for writing 'a scandalous & dangerous paper against his Majesty and Government'.[38] Finally, we now have quite firm evidence that some northern Quakers were involved in plotting an uprising against Charles II, the so-called Northern Plot of 1663.[39]

A recent book by J.R. Jacob has alerted us to the fact that radical ideas survived the Restoration, nurtured by figures like Henry Stubbe who 'continued, often by resort to subterfuge, to preach a message subversive of Restoration orthodoxy'.[40] Possibly future work on the Quakers will discover similar survival and subterfuge. When we probe beneath the level of the printed pamphlet, we find John Brown, who in 1664 entered a meeting at the Bull and Mouth in London, his hair cropped and covered in dust, and naked except for a loin-cloth. This bizarre symbolism was clearly seditious. God 'will cut of ye locks of ye head, & shave ye Crowne', Brown predicted, with obvious reference to the King; 'Woe to C & J [Charles and James, Duke of York] destruction draweth Nye'.[41] Or we find the poem of the Quaker William Smith, penned about the time of the Northern Plot of 1663:

> A Crown a Throne, a Scepter is but the world renown
> and when this Man honour'd is, yet soon he must come down
> There is no Safety in them, tho' Man in them Depend
> But down they must into the dust, & none shall them defend.

He concluded (the emphasis is mine):

> Let him yt readeth Understand
> for certainly the time's at hand
> wherein great wonders shall be Seen,
> such as of late years have not been

And who enquires when this shall be,
or when they may this come to see
Let time and Years speak as they Come
in *Sixty Thre much will be done*.[42]

But Brown and Smith were not typical of post-1660 Quakerism. As the evidence stands, it seems unlikely that the Quakers were significant carriers of radical ideas. By and large, the militant edge of Quakerism was blunted after the Revolution. The important point about the Northern Plot is the *lack* of Quaker support. The majority of Friends became pacifists; they were no longer a threat. When the 'Good Old Cause' was championed by Monmouth in 1685, few Quakers (we know only of twelve, three of whom were executed) turned out in support.[43]

There were other changes to the political side of Quakerism during this period. In the 1650s the movement had been poised on the brink of a genuine radical egalitarianism: in the 1660s and 1670s it drew back. Robert Barclay declared in his *Apology* of 1678:

> Let not any judge, that from our opinion . . . any necessity of Levelling will follow, or that all Men must have things in Common . . . we say not hereby that no Man may use the Creation more or less than another: For we know, that as it hath pleased God to dispense it diversly, giving to some more, and some less, so they may use it accordingly. . . . let the Brother of high degree rejoice in that he is abased, and such as God calls in low degree, to be content with their Condition, not envying those Brethren, who have greater abundance, knowing they have received abundance as to the inward Man; which is chiefly to be regarded.[44]

Weighty Friends of the early eighteenth century were to proclaim their attachment to the doctrine of the 'Great Chain of Being', 'the true honour and obedience due from Subjects to their Prince, inferiors to superiors, from Children to Parents, and Servants to Masters, whereby the mutual relations, betwixt those different Ranks and Degrees of men, have been and are asserted and endeavoured to be established after the manner that our Saviour and his Apostles were pleased to direct.'[45]

Political radicalism appeared to revive from time to time. The charter for Quaker West New Jersey, drawn up in 1677, seemed to embody many of the radical demands of earlier years. Power was to be vested in a single legislative assembly, elected annually by an extremely liberal franchise. There was to be trial by jury, and 'all persons' were to have 'free liberty' to plead their 'own cause'. Justices and local office holders were to be elected. Religious freedom was guaranteed. 'We lay a foundation for after ages to understand their liberty as men and christians, that they may not be brought in bondage, but by their own consent; for we put the power in the people', wrote Billing and his fellow trustees.[46] In the colony of Pennsylvania, however, only half the adult male population had the vote, and power was concentrated in a council (or upper house) and governor – men 'most eminent for vertue Wisdom and Substance'. The 'Number of Knowing men is ever least in any Country', William Penn replied to criticisms that the Pennsylvania Assembly was a mere cipher. He wanted to avoid 'ye confusion of a multitude'.[47]

In England, as Thomas O'Malley has shown, Quaker central organization – the Second Day Morning Meeting and the Meeting for Sufferings – stifled political speculation and killed the aggressive remnants of the 1650s.[48] The minutes kept by these bodies show prospective pamphlets being laid aside, because 'it was judged not a convenient season to make it publick', or it was 'neither safe for him nor Truth to Publish it', or it was 'not a fitt time to Print much upon yt Accot'.[49] Quaker self-censorship did the state's job for it in the 1670s and 1680s. Technically, as O'Malley puts it, the illegal Quaker press was defying the government, but the political content of the books which it produced during that period was 'not provocative': 'if anything it was supplicatory'.[50] In terms of actual output of individual titles, Quaker pamphleteering peaked from 1658 to 1662; thereafter it dropped by half or more, rising during times of crisis but never recapturing the output of the early years.[51]

IV

Quaker censorship also curbed religious enthusiasm. Gone was the imperative to engage in sectarian debate. In 1674 the Second Day Morning Meeting refused to publish a tract directed at the Baptists because 'as the Case now stands betweene the Bapts & Friends They would not willingly have other Controversyes brought in to make more worke'. Another manuscript was rejected in 1682 because the Quaker elite did not want to revive old quarrels and 'raise new disputes'.[52]

We still do not know enough about the long-term development of Quaker theology to reach any firm conclusions about the period after 1660.[53] Certainly doctrine was systematized for the first time in the 1670s, in the work of the university-educated Robert Barclay, whose *Catechism and Confession of Faith* (1673) and *Apology* (1678) became the official Quaker statements of faith. But a copy of Barclay in every Quaker meeting house and many a Quaker home did not ensure erudition or doctrinal conformity. Helen Forde's work on Derbyshire meeting libraries during the early eighteenth century hardly indicates a thirst for theology: the more avid readers borrowed eight books in ten years, ten books in nineteen years, and twelve in eight years.[54] George Keith, who led a schism in Pennsylvania in the 1690s, complained in 1688 that American Quakers were 'too little acquainted and known in the Holy Scriptures', and that too many ignored or neglected the historical Christ, 'his outward Coming, and what he did and suffered for us in the Flesh'. Keith suggested the need for even greater systematization: sect members should be asked to demonstrate their commitment to a formalized creed.[55]

After 1660 official Quakerism quietly dropped the perfectionist claims of earlier years. Perfection was now a slow process, no sudden event corresponding to conversion.[56] Among the 'errors' Keith detected in his co-religionists in the early 1690s was the belief that 'Christ mends soules perfectly at once so as to have no sin'.[57] Enthusiasm waned gradually. In 1662 Quaker women had symbolically poured blood over the altar in St Paul's; but in 1700 when a Chester Quaker proclaimed truth in the streets and Cathedral and was imprisoned for his trouble, he was rebuked by the Second Day Morning Meeting.[58] By the end of the seventeenth century fasting was forbidden; dreams and 'pretended visions' had to be approved by meetings.[59] Thomas Ellwood spent his final years scrubbing George Fox's more enthusiastic reminiscences out of the first edition of the *Journal*.[60] And George Whitehead was able to atone for the over-zealousness of youth, through judicious use of the editor's quill.[61]

As hinted earlier, this change in spirit was reflected in the sect's meetings for worship. Meeting houses gradually replaced what Richard Vann has called the 'inspired casualness'[62] of the first decade with its great open-air gatherings. By the 1690s women and men sat in different parts of the room in the meetings for worship, just as they did in Anglican churches, and Quaker 'ministers' (the 'Public Friends') sat separately in a kind of gallery.[63] The spontaneous, enthusiastic, incantatory style of the early Quaker preacher, Richard Bauman suggests, was replaced by a more rigid, authoritarian, catechetical technique: hearers were being questioned to mentally produce answers *already known* by the questioner': in the relationship between minister and audience the emphasis was now on subordination rather than collaboration.[64] In the 1650s Burrough had stood on a bench in the Bull and Mouth with a Bible in his hand, the place in an uproar; there had been wailing and trembling. In 1691 the Huntingdonshire Monthly Meeting found it necessary to speak to Francis Field 'as touching her procedure in an opposit and wilfull opening her mouth in a meeting too Largly at many times'.[65] A Yearly Meeting questionnaire in 1706 asked 'Do Friends give way to sleep in meetings?' By 1720 the Colchester meeting had appointed monitors to awaken offenders.[66] The Seekers had become sleepers.

v

Although northern Quakerism had a rudimentary organizational structure during the Interregnum, it was not really until 1667 that, under the guidance of Fox, full-scale organization began. By the 1670s the Society of Friends had a nation-wide system of local, regional, and national business meetings – the Yearly Meeting, Meeting for Sufferings, Second Day Morning Meeting, Six Weeks' Meeting, Quarterly Meetings, Monthly Meetings, and various separate Women's Meetings.[67]

Historians have been understandably impressed by the democratic implications of seventeenth-century sectarianism. 'They [Baptists and Quakers] were able to create a system of democratic representative assemblies with no previous parallel, at least in English history', each sect 'a voluntary association of free and equal members, united in opposition to the doctrines, practices, and moral discipline of the national church and, by implication, of the social system whose values that church expressed.'[68] But by the second generation of sectarian membership this was no longer the case. Quaker children were born into the sect. For them there was no 'free contract'; they were subject to catechizing and enculturation much in the way that they would be as members of the Church of England.[69] Through its system of business meetings the Quaker movement soon developed its own 'ruling class'. Quarterly Meetings in Leicestershire were effectively run by a small number of local families, a handful of names 'which from father to son and grandson . . . formed the select Quaker leadership'.[70] In Buckinghamshire and Norfolk the Quaker ministry and those who attended Monthly Meetings were men with the leisure and the means to govern the sect: a few gentry, professional men, yeomen, and wholesale traders. Richard Vann has found that the rank and file of the Quaker movement became more plebeian as the sect entered the eighteenth century. But control of the sect, in the form of the meetings for business and discipline, was in the hands of the Quaker bourgeoisie.[71]

One is struck by an unavoidable sense of irony when reading the disciplinary records of the Society of Friends. Those who had said that they 'cared not for any Ecclesiastical power' were engaged in a wide-ranging system of self-discipline. Granted, it was voluntary discipline – they had been 'brought in bondage . . . by their own consent', as Billing might have put it – but it was control nevertheless. The Quaker community replaced the local community, dictating its own social rules; with a message even for those 'troubled with wind'.[72] As it became organized, the movement assumed something of the role of the once-hated church courts, with visitors, visitations,[73] and, in Somerset, market-place penance for an erring sect member.[74] Not surprisingly, some Somerset Friends compared Quaker organization to 'the Bishop's Court'.[75]

Quakers were 'the royal seed of God', drawn apart from the corrupt world. Their lives were to be testimonies to their spiritual separation and thus required a high standard of moral conduct. Internal disputes, however trifling, were believed to reflect badly on the movement. Quarrels were 'in breach of that brotherly Love which ought to be held and practised amongst Christian brethren'.[76] Taking legal action against a co-religionist was frowned upon as 'a publick reproach & reflection on the profession of friends',[77] so Monthly Meetings were quite often intervening in and arbitrating arguments between Quakers: disagreements over debts, property, wills, business deals, and in one case the felling of some trees.[78]

As an alternative society, the sect was responsible for the moral welfare of its members – always with an eye to its reputation in the outside world. Much of the business of Monthly and Quarterly Meetings was devoted to the close supervision of marriage within the Society. Prospective marriage partners had to declare their intentions (the equivalent of the publishing of banns), parents or guardians had to indicate their approval, and local meetings had to certify that bride and groom were clear of other affective commitments. The meeting would also make sure that both partners were versed in Quaker beliefs and practice. Marriage to first or second cousins or in-laws was not encouraged.[79] Widows and widowers had to allow a decent interval between the death of a spouse and remarriage.[80] Marriage to 'those of the world' was anathema; indeed, one of the functions of meetings was to discourage the development of such relationships. Nevertheless, perhaps the greatest disciplinary problem of meetings was marriage outside the Society.[81]

Sexual intercourse on promise of marriage seems to have been common plebeian practice in early modern England. Quaker meetings took disciplinary action against those who cohabited before marriage, but there is enough evidence in meeting minutes to show that it was a recurrent problem for the sect. In 1672 the London Six Weeks' Meeting felt impelled to 'draw up a Testimony against such young Men & young women as intending a Marriage do go & dwell or Lodge in one House together, before the Matter of Marriage is aproved & Finisht'; while in 1686 Somerset Friends were warned against 'letting out their affections one to another so inordinately before a proposeall be made to friends', and 'liveing togeather in one house or famely or too much frequenting each others company while under a concerne of marriage'.[82]

Supervision did not end with the marriage declaration. Saints were to behave soberly, an example to the world. Disorderly marriages were counselled; persistent wife-beaters were disowned.[83] However, organized Quakerism did not encourage marital separation. Isaac and Joan Bryant of Shepton Mallet in Somersetshire 'lived a contentious life for many years'. Isaac, a husbandman, had left his wife to go to West New Jersey for five years. Upon his return the 'contention & strife' had continued, so he had 'cast her off with all his children (one excepted) & refused to give or allow them mayntenance'. The Somerset Quarterly

Meeting decided that while neither partner was blameless the main fault lay with Isaac; yet they still considered that the couple 'ought not to separate . . . But ought to dwell together in the feare of god as man & wife during life'.[84]

Quaker discipline was remarkably gentle by seventeenth-century standards. Every effort was made to reclaim an errant sect member. Individual offenders were counselled over and over again, and Friends could be extremely persevering. John Pinkerd was approached by a deputation from the North Somerset Monthly Meeting in 1683 for his 'irregular takeing of a wife'. At first he would not admit to his mistake; but the delegates kept visiting him from August 1683 until he eventually agreed in July 1685 that he had done wrong in marrying contrary to the conventions of the movement.[85] A testimony of self-condemnation would avoid disownment, which was issued only as a last resort. Public condemnation, as the minutes of the Men's Meeting in Bristol state for 1669, came only after 'foure or five exhortations'.[86]

The criterion for membership was unity with the sect – as defined by the Quaker bureaucracy. Quaker backsliders were 'not truely subjected to ye teachings of the Pure spirit of God, or light, or life, or Grace . . . wch teaches to deny all ungodlinesse and worldly Lusts, and to live soberly'.[87] An unrepentant backslider or a particularly grievous offender had, by 'his actions', demonstrated that he was not truly of the Society of Friends, was not 'of us', had never in fact been a real Quaker.[88] This idea of an 'invisible membership'[89] permeates Quaker statements at the time of the Monmouth rebellion, when George Whitehead said of a co-religionist involved in the rising, 'he has *ipso facto* gone from truth & rendred himself no real Quaker, Ceasing by ye same fact to be one of us or in society with us', and when some Somerset Quakers wrote of others implicated in the troubles, 'severall of them long before ye sd Insurecon, their bad conversacons had manifested them to be wholly gon from our society; tho they might retaine ye name of Quaker'.[90] Occasionally the name of an apostate was erased from the meeting minute books: it was as if he or she had never existed.[91]

As an alternative society, the sect was also responsible for the material welfare of its members. Meetings intervened in the economic life of Friends in various ways, providing aid to fire victims in a pre-insurance age,[92] backing small traders during times of hardship (weeding out persistent failures), and always keeping an eye on the indebtedness of Quaker tradesmen. Help was selective. Those like the two Somerset Quakers, one of whom got into difficulties through his involvement in 'matters . . . to high for him' and the other of whom ended up in debt because of 'extravagant dealings . . . in buying & selling of Cattle, & farmying of great estates', could expect little sympathy.[93]

The emphasis in Quakerism was on works – not in the Roman Catholic sense of justification and propitiation, but in the Weberian sense of a mark of divine favour. Works flowed from grace, an exaggeration and development of a tendency already implicit in Calvinism.[94] 'A good Tree cannot bring forth evill fruit, nor a corrupt Tree bring forth good fruit.'[95] Frugality, simplicity (and thus accumulation?), productivity, industry, were signs of divine approval: extravagance, luxury, idleness, non-productive and destructive wealth were the marks of Cain and Lucifer. Be 'not churlish, cross, stubborn, nor slothful in business; but fervent in Spirit, serving the Lord . . . knowing that of the Lord you shall receive a reward'.[96] (Nathaniel Smith, a former Quaker, said that the 'simple People' took the sect's prosperity to be a sign of divine favour.[97])

This stress on works had implications for the movement's arrangements for the relief of poorer members. The industrious poor, and those who had fallen on hard times through no fault of their own, were cushioned; the idle, the profligate, were not. The Bristol Men's Meeting provided coal and cheese for the poor during the winter of 1667, they gave Widow Bowen 40s. to recover her bed out of pawn, and in the 1690s they set up a workhouse 'to imploy poore friends at worke, in weaveing &c'. But when a Quaker inmate of the workhouse misbehaved, they put him out for 'loose & idle liveing'.[98] The West Somerset Monthly Meeting supported the lame Burnham widow, Susan Petheram, and her four children for some fourteen years, paying her rent (the money paid to her was always held in trust), getting in turf for her for the winter, and organizing apprenticeships for her sons. They helped John Hardy who had four small children, another on the way, and a wife 'in childbed', 'all depending on his single labour'. They aided a Quaker who was dimsighted and another who was out of work. But when they were approached by Eleanor Collins, a poor alehouse-keeper, they first wanted to

know how she 'doth employ her selfe'.[99] Ideally, people were
helped to help themselves. Families were rescued from a future of
deprivation by channelling their children (boys and girls) into
apprenticeships. Thus, as Fox explained to the Berkshire
Quarterly Meeting, the youth concerned would eventually be in
the position to 'helpe his Mother and father, and Reare up the
familye that is decayed . . . and be a meanes to take off
Incumberance off your Selves'.[100]

VI

In many respects, the Quaker 'middling sort', with their war
against sin and inculcation of godliness, stood firmly in the
tradition of the Puritan 'reformation of manners'.[101] Quakers fell
foul of their meetings for a variety of offences, a brief list of which
gives some idea of the godly impulse: for 'being often overtaken
with drinking, or being drunk', for 'lewd conversacion', for
'playing cards & drinking more then is meete at Warminster', for
'being overcome in drink quarrelling and strikeing', for being at a
playhouse, for playing 'Shuffleboard (as they call it) upon
London Road', for 'keeping bad company, and for drinking and
singing like lewd women, att one Johnsons house an Inn-keeper
in Q. Camell on one of those days called Easter holy-days', for
'neglecting meetings', for 'going togeather before marriage', for
'keeping company' with 'one Lews Ryder a Butcher & a bad
man', for 'Keeping company with a woman of the world att
unseasonable times & in a lose and lycentious manner', for being
'given to Cards, dancing, fives playing and other heathenish
practices', for 'begeting Clare Key with child, haveing a wife of
his owne', for 'adulterous practices', for keeping a woman 'in his
house as wife', for 'lying wth each other before the publication of
Marriage'.[102]

Seventeenth-century Quakerism contained the seeds of a
genuine, godly subculture, adopting, adapting, and rejecting the
values of the dominant and subordinate cultures. It is the culture
of the Protestant middling sort, hostile towards the customs and
habits of traditional popular culture – 'throwing at Cocks and
going to Cockaynes'[103] – yet dismissive, as we have seen in
various parts of this volume, of many of the trappings of gentry
dominance. Quaker culture was serious culture, with no time for
the frivolity and self-indulgence of drama, painting, sculpture,
music, and dance, or the even less serious forms of popular

leisure. 'How many plays did Jesus Christ and his apostles recreate themselves at? What poets, romances, comedies, and the like did the apostles and saints make or use to pass away their time withal?'[104] In a celebrated incident in London in the 1650s, Burrough stepped into a wrestling ring and lectured the watching apprentices and journeymen on the vanity of the sport.[105] When he turned Quaker, the music teacher Solomon Eccles 'burnt and broke many good Instruments of Musick'.[106] A succession of Friends were to look back in horror at a pre-Quaker youth spent in 'excess of drinking, eating, and wicked singing, and idle jestings, and foolish laughter', 'vain Sports and Pastimes, as Ringing, Dancing, and the like', 'Wrestling, Lea[p]ing, Football playing and going to Horse Races'.[107] The Yorkshire Quaker John Hall (1637-1719) was said to have 'kept an Inn at Skipton for the Space of thirteen years, and kept his Authority nobly in the Truth, while in that Place, not allowing Drunkenness, Singing, Dancing, Musick or Excess in his House, but bearing his Testimony faithfully against Intemperance'.[108]

Quaker culture was also Protestant culture, rejecting the ritual and imagery of the old religion for the equally powerful symbolism of the new. In 1659 Thomas Hart called for the removal of the 'smell of popery' from England, for the erasure of the 'Pope's image', the cross, which was still to be found on churches, weights and measures, ships, taverns, and coats of arms.[109] Quakers removed the 'St' from St Ives and Bury St Edmunds; they rejected the Latin names of the months for January to August and the names of the days of the week, using numbers instead. Some were even against the woodcut prints found on broadside ballads, because they were held to be in violation of the second commandment.[110] When the Leveller leader John Lilburne was given a Quaker funeral in 1657, not even a hearse-cloth covered his coffin, which was carried, unadorned, through the streets of London.[111]

And Quaker culture was plain culture: simplicity, lack of ornamentation, in language and prose,[112] in furniture, architecture, gardens, and dress.[113] It is possible to capture the Quaker aesthetic in a series of images: the simple declaration of a Quaker wedding; the plain Quaker coffin in an unmarked Bristol grave;[114] the portrait of the departed, preserved, not on canvas, but in the simple, black-on-white profile of the Quaker silhouette.[115]

And yet a coherent, godly culture was never attained. In Quakerism, as in the world, there was tension between the 'rough' and the 'respectable'. The so-called 'Proud Quakers' of Nottingham, followers of Rhys Johns (or Rice Jones), an alehouse-keeper who was perhaps the first Quaker to secede from the movement, were said to be 'the greatest football players and wrestlers in the country', and they met on Sundays 'to play at shovell board'.[116] The very presence of the fighting, fornicating, drunken Quakers mentioned earlier, Quakers who married outside the movement, who went to Cockaynes, and who threw at cocks reveals that at the end of the seventeenth century many of the Quaker rank and file were not too far removed from the culture of plebeian England. The sect's cultural limitations reflected their social diversity, the tensions within that social category, 'the middling sort'. The Quaker aesthetic was threatened from above as well as from below. Meetings had to warn against 'all pride & Vanity in Apparell, Rufled Phantasticall & high dreses, Gaudy attire, flowerd & Striped Silks of divers Coulers', 'Broidered haire or pearls or Gold or Costly Array', 'long lapp'd Sleeves or Coates gathered at the Sides, or Superfluous Buttons, or Broad Ribbons about their Hatts, or long curled Perriwiggs'; 'Likewise Vaine & Superfluous furniture, and things yt are for Ostentation & Pride more than Service in their houses'.[117] Philadelphia merchants were able to salve their consciences and maintain their social position by buying clothing and furniture – 'of the best Sort but Plain'.[118]

VII

The Toleration Act was passed in 1689, closing a chapter in Quaker history. Quakers were still prosecuted for their refusal to pay tithes; but the prosecution rate was much lower than it had been in the early years, and many Friends were now actively conniving in tithe payment and, in some cases, receiving tithes.[119] By the end of the century, the Quakers had adjusted to the state and the state had adjusted to them. When an anti-Quaker agitator asked some MPs to do something about Quakerism, he was told that it was a matter for clerics.[120] Once feared as symptomatic of a growing social radicalism, the 'Fanatick agitations' and 'enthusiastic rants' of a Nayler, a Fox, were put down to 'impulses of a warm brain', and the writer, a doctor, recommended the discipline of a madhouse.[121] In the mid-seventeenth century men had been turned off their land for their Quakerism: by the eighteenth century, Irish landlords were *looking for* Quaker tenants for their farms because they were careful husbandmen and reliable with the rent.[122]

It is easier to chart the transformation of Quakerism after 1660 than it is to account for it. The impact of wider political events was crucial. The restoration of monarchy in 1660 almost forced pacifism upon the sect, partly through disillusionment, partly because of the simple need to survive; the first declarations of pacifism came with the assault on Quakerism in 1660 and 1661. Indeed, we should not be too surprised at the difference between a movement on the attack and a sect under siege. The death of so many of the early personalities during the first two decades of the movement had a devastating effect. Of those who appear in this book, Thomas Aldam, George Bishop, Edward Burrough, John Camm, William Caton, Richard Farnworth, Samuel Fisher, George Fox the younger, Joseph Fuce, Thomas Holme, Francis Howgil, Richard Hubberthorne, John Lilburne, James Milner, James Nayler, Benjamin Nicholson, James Parnell, Anthony Pearson, Edward Pyott, Richard Sale, Martha Simmonds, Humphrey Smith, Amos Stoddart, and William Woodcock were dead by 1670. The removal of radicals like Bishop, Burrough, Fox the younger, Hubberthorne, Nicholson, Parnell, and Smith left the movement to men like George Whitehead and Thomas Salthouse, and to the influences of the patrician Penn and Barclay. The struggle to survive Restoration persecution encouraged organization, and organization stimulated conservatism.[123] The need to survive also fed the drive towards respectability, for Fox, in particular, was always sensitive about the sect's image in the hostile world.

Yet it was not simply a case of a movement denied the chance to create a godly world turning inwards to create its own little commonwealth. The Quakers were influenced by events in the wider society, but they shaped their own destinies too. For, as I suggested at the beginning of this chapter, Quaker organization, self-censorship, self-discipline, built on tendencies already present: it represented, if you like, the logic of the godly impulse. It was perhaps inevitable that the anarchical implications of the doctrine of the light within would have to be tempered by some form of group control if the movement was to avoid fragmentation into a thousand competing faiths. The light within taught John Perrot to keep his hat on, even before his God; it persuaded William Salt that meetings should not be held 'without the immediate leadings of the Spirit of the Lord'.[124] The problem, as a Quaker put it in 1659, was to distinguish 'truth from Imaginations'.[125] The answer in the 1660s and 1670s was that the leadings within each individual had to be weighed against the light within the godly community. 'God hath ordinarily, in communicating of his will . . . employed such whom he made use of in gathering his church', wrote Barclay in *The Anarchy of the Ranters* (1674): and they, as Fox pointed out in a different context, were the 'weighty, seasoned, and substantial Friends that understands the business of the Church'.[126] Any movement born of revolution must change to meet the needs of a new generation. The light within spoke differently to the Quaker merchants of London, Bristol, Dublin, and Philadelphia, and to the other bourgeois Friends who increasingly controlled the sect.

Notes

ABBREVIATIONS

The place of publication in all notes is London unless otherwise stated.

Acts and Ordinances   *Acts and Ordinances of the Interregnum 1642-1660*, ed. C. H. Firth and R. S. Rait (3 vols, 1911)

Barbour, *Quakers*   H. Barbour, *The Quakers in Puritan England* (New Haven, 1964)

Besse   J. Besse, *A Collection of the Sufferings of the People called Quakers* (2 vols, 1753)

BL   British Library

Book of Miracles   *George Fox's 'Book of Miracles'*, ed. H. J. Cadbury (NY, 1973 reprint)

Braithwaite, *Beginnings*   W. C. Braithwaite, *The Beginnings of Quakerism* (Cambridge, 1970 edn)

Braithwaite, *Second Period*   W. C. Braithwaite, *The Second Period of Quakerism* (Cambridge, 1961 edn)

Capp, *Fifth Monarchy Men*   B. S. Capp, *The Fifth Monarchy Men* (1972)

Clarendon MS.   Clarendon Manuscripts, Bodleian Library, Oxford

Cole, 'Quakers and the English Revolution'   W. A. Cole, 'The Quakers and the English Revolution', in T. Aston (ed.), *Crisis in Europe* (1970 edn)

Cole, 'Quakers and Politics'   W. A. Cole, 'The Quakers and Politics, 1652-1660' (Univ. of Cambridge Ph.D. thesis, 1955)

CSP	*Calendar of State Papers, Domestic Series*
Diary of Ralph Josselin	*The Diary of Ralph Josselin 1616-1683*, ed. A. Macfarlane (1976)
Diary of Thomas Burton	*The Diary of Thomas Burton*, ed. J. T. Rutt (4 vols, 1828)
Extracts	*Extracts from State Papers*, ed. N. Penney (1913)
FHL	Friends House Library, London
FPT	*The First Publishers of Truth*, ed. N. Penney (1907)
GBS	Great Book of Sufferings Manuscripts, Friends House Library, London
HMC	*Historical Manuscripts Commission*
JEH	*Journal of Ecclesiastical History*
JFHS	*Journal of the Friends Historical Society*
JGF	*The Journal of George Fox*, ed. N. Penney (2 vols, NY, 1973 reprint)
JRH	*Journal of Religious History*
MMB(1)	*Minute Book of the Men's Meeting of the Society of Friends in Bristol 1667-1686* (Bristol Record Society, xxvi, 1971)
MMB(2)	*Minute Book of the Men's Meeting of the Society of Friends in Bristol 1686-1704* (Bristol Record Society, xxx, 1977)
NY	New York
P. and P.	*Past and Present*
PRO	Public Record Office
QH	*Quaker History*

QS	Quarter Sessions
RDM	K. Thomas, *Religion and the Decline of Magic* (1973 edn)
Reay, 'Early Quaker Activity'	B. G. Reay, 'Early Quaker activity and reactions to it, 1652-1664' (Univ. of Oxford D. Phil. thesis, 1979)
RO	Record Office
SQM	*The Somersetshire Quarterly Meeting of the Society of Friends 1668-1699* (Somerset Record Society, lxxv, 1978)
Thurloe	*A Collection of the State Papers of John Thurloe*, ed. T. Birch (7 vols, 1742)
Vann, *Social Development*	R. T. Vann, *The Social Development of English Quakerism 1655-1755* (Cambridge, Mass., 1969)
WTUD	C. Hill, *The World Turned Upside Down* (1972 edn)

INTRODUCTION

1. *WTUD*; J. F. C. Harrison, *The Second Coming. Popular Millenarianism 1780-1850* (1979).

2. *WTUD*, 11.

3. J. F. Maclear, 'Quakerism and the end of the Interregnum', *Church History*, xix (1950). For the others, see Abbreviations above.

4. D. E. C. Eversley, 'The Demography of the Irish Quakers, 1650-1850', in J. M. Goldstrom and L. A. Clarkson (eds), *Irish Population, Economy, and Society* (Oxford, 1981), ch. 3.

5. B. Levy, 'The Birth of the "Modern Family" in Early America', in M. W. Zuckerman (ed.), *Friends and Neighbors* (Philadelphia, 1982), 56.

6. R. Bauman, 'Aspects of 17th Century Quaker Rhetoric', *Quarterly Journal of Speech*, lvi (1970), 74. And see now Bauman's *Let your words be few. Symbolism of speaking and*

silence among seventeenth-century Quakers (Cambridge, 1983). Unfortunately Bauman's book appeared after I had completed my typescript, but I was still able to make some use of it.

7. G. F. Nuttall, *Studies in Christian Enthusiasm* (Wallingford, 1948), 13; Barbour, *Quakers*, xi.

8. B. Manning, *The English People and the English Revolution* (1976).

I BIRTH OF A MOVEMENT

1. *Journal of George Fox*, ed. J. L. Nickalls (Cambridge, 1952), 8-9.

2. Ibid, 7, 11; *JGF*, i.27.

3. *Journal of George Fox*, ed. Nickalls, 34, 33, 27.

4. Ibid, 27.

5. Barbour, *Quakers*, 153.

6. *Journal of George Fox*, ed. Nickalls, 40.

7. For this milieu, see J. F. McGregor, 'Seekers and Ranters', in J. F. McGregor and B. Reay (eds), *Radical Religion in the English Revolution* (Oxford, 1984), ch. 5 (p. 128 for the quotation).

8. Vann, *Social Development*, 9; L. Muggleton, *The Acts of the Witnesses of the Spirit* (1764), 151.

9. Braithwaite, *Beginnings*, 62.

10. PRO, Assi 45/4/3/103-8.

11. See Cole, 'Quakers and Politics'.

12. Braithwaite, *Beginnings*, 57, 131-2, 308, 311.

13. Ibid, 71-2, and pp. 36, 69-70 below.

14. Ibid, 75.

15.	B. G. Blackwood, 'Agrarian Unrest and the Early Lancashire Quakers', *JFHS*, li (1965), 72-6.

16.	B. Reay, 'Quaker Opposition to Tithes 1652-1660', *P. and P.*, 86 (1980), 100, 103-4.

17.	Braithwaite, *Beginnings*, 193-4.

18.	Vann, *Social Development*, 83-4. Vann also calculated ages for the early northern converts, but his sample was smaller than mine.

19.	FHL, William Caton MS. iii. 137-47, 155-8; 'Swarthmore MS. Letters of John Audland', ed. C. Horle (typescript, FHL, 1975), no. 18; C. W. Horle, 'John Camm', *QH*, lxx (1981), 77.

20.	G. F. Nuttall, *James Nayler: a Fresh Approach* (1954), 10-13; *Letters of Early Friends*, ed. A. R. Barclay (1841), 37, 53-4, 59-60.

21.	W. Prynne, *The Quakers Unmasked* (1655), 36.

22.	Braithwaite, *Beginnings*; Barbour, *Quakers*. See also R. Bauman, *Let your words be few* (Cambridge, 1983), ch. 5.

23.	*JGF*, i. 404.

24.	Ibid, ii. 460.

25.	For the numbers of pamphlets, see D. Runyon, 'Types of Quaker Writings by Year – 1650–1699', in *Early Quaker Writings*, ed. H. Barbour and A. Roberts (Grand Rapids, 1973), 568-9.

26.	Barbour, *Quakers*, 182.

27.	Capp, *Fifth Monarchy Men*, 79.

28.	Vann, *Social Development*, 199.

29.	J. F. McGregor, 'The Baptists: Fount of All Heresy', in McGregor and Reay (eds), *Radical Religion*, 34.

30.	See ch. 6 below.

31.   Braithwaite, *Beginnings*, ch. 13.

32.   FHL, MS. Portfolio xxxvi.149.

33.   Vann, *Social Development*, 199.

34.   N. P. Tanner (ed.), *Heresy Trials in the Diocese of Norwich* (1977), 10-22; C. Cross, *Church and People 1450-1660* (Glasgow, 1976), chs 1-2; J. F. Davis, 'Lollardy and the Reformation in England', *Archiv Für Reformationsgeschichte*, lxxiii (1982).

35.   A. Hamilton, *The Family of Love* (Cambridge, 1981), ch. 6; J. W. Martin, 'Elizabethan Familists and English Separatism', *Journal of British Studies*, xx, no. 1 (1980).

36.   D. Loades, 'Anabaptism and English Sectarianism in the Mid-Sixteenth Century', *Studies in Church History: Subsidia*, 2 (1979); M. Tolmie, *The Triumph of the Saints* (Cambridge, 1977), ch. 1, 69-72.

37.   See *WTUD*; and McGregor and Reay (eds), *Radical Religion*. The Muggletonian quotation comes from C. Hill, B. Reay, and W. Lamont, *The World of the Muggletonians* (1983), 19.

38.   For a slightly more detailed summary, see B. Reay, 'Radicalism and Religion in the English Revolution', in McGregor and Reay (eds), *Radical Religion*, ch. 1.

39.   J. Morrill, 'The Church in England, 1642-9', in Morrill (ed.), *Reactions to the English Civil War 1642-1649* (1982), ch. 4.

40.   Vann, *Social Development*, 22.

41.   *Journal of George Fox*, ed. Nickalls, 4-9.

42.   G. Rofe, *The Righteousness of God to Man* (1656), 14-15.

43.   *A short History of the Life of John Crook* (1706), 9.

44.   H. Clark, *A Rod Discover'd* (1659), 36; J. Stalham, *The Reviler Rebuked* (1657), sig. D2; C. R. Simpson, 'Benjamin Furly and his Library', *JFHS*, xi (1914), 73; M. B. Endy, *William Penn and Early Quakerism* (Princeton, 1973), 121; J. L. Nickalls, 'George Fox's Library', *JFHS*, xxviii (1931), 4, 8; G. F. Nuttall,

The Holy Spirit in Puritan Faith and Experience (Oxford, 1946), 13, n. 2, 184 addendum.

45. Simpson, op. cit., 73; L. Muggleton, *A Looking-Glass for George Fox* (1756), 10; Nuttall, *Holy Spirit*, 16-18; F. E[llington], *Christian Information Concerning these Last Times* (1664), 10ff.; J. Whiting, *Persecution Expos'd* (1715), 187; *Jacob Boehme Society Quarterly*, i, no. 8 (1954), 32; FHL, MS. Morning Meeting Minutes 1673-92, pp. 1-2.

46. Nuttall, *James Nayler*.

47. F. Heal, 'The Family of Love and the Diocese of Ely', *Studies in Church History*, ix (1972); M. Spufford, *Contrasting Communities* (Cambridge, 1974), 256-7, 284, 351.

48. E. Lewis Evans, 'Morgan Llwyd and the Early Friends', *Friends' Quarterly*, viii (1954), 50, 54; *idem*, 'Morgan Lloyd and Jacob Boehme', *Jacob Boehme Society Quarterly*, i, no. 4 (1953), 13, 14, 15; *WTUD*, 154; T. Richards, *Religious Developments in Wales (1654-1662)* (1923), 265-6; R. Farmer, *Sathan Inthron'd* (1657), 17, 46-7; Stalham, *Reviler Rebuked*, sig. D4v.

49. *WTUD*, 193; Horle, 'John Camm', 79.

50. Vann, *Social Development*, 10-11; 'Swarthmore MS. Letters of John Audland', no. 18.

51. G. F. Nuttall, *The Welsh Saints* (Cardiff, 1957), ch. 4; Vann, *Social Development*, 23-7; C. W. Horle, 'Quakers and Baptists 1647-1660', *Baptist Quarterly*, xxvi (1976); Braithwaite, *Beginnings*, index: Seekers; J. F. McGregor, 'Ranterism and the Development of Early Quakerism', *JRH*, ix (1977); Capp, *Fifth Monarchy Men*, 223-4.

52. Spufford, *Contrasting Communities*, 283.

53. A. Macfarlane, *The Family Life of Ralph Josselin* (Cambridge, 1970), 26; *Diary of Ralph Josselin*, 271, 348.

54. Reay, 'Quaker Opposition to Tithes'.

55. A. Woolrych, *Commonwealth to Protectorate* (Oxford, 1982), 119, 178, 191-2.

56. Reay, 'Early Quaker Activity', 66-7.

57. D. Underdown, *Somerset in the Civil War and Interregnum* (1973), 186; *Calendar of the Proceedings of the Committee for Compounding* (1967), 171, 194, 196, 201, 211, 226, 247, 281, 289, 369, 381, 395, 488, 517, 524, 679, 815, 3025; A. H. Dodd, *Studies in Stuart Wales* (Cardiff, 1971), 113-14, 147-8.

58. M. Kishlansky, 'The Creation of the New Model Army', *P. and P.*, 81 (1978).

59. I owe this observation to Mr J. F. McGregor.

60. Braithwaite, *Beginnings*, 61.

61. Vann, *Social Development*, 14.

62. *To the Generals, and Captains, Officers, and Souldiers of this present Army* [1657], 2.

63. See ch. 3 below, n. 12.

64. *JGF*, i. 32, 402.

65. FHL, Swarthmore MS. i. 373.

66. *JGF*, i. 423, 454; FHL, Swarthmore MS. iv. 141; *Records of the Churches of Christ*, ed. E. B. Underhill (1854), 330-31.

67. Farmer, *Sathan Inthron'd*, 56.

68. G. Whitehead, *The Christian Progress of that Ancient Servant* (1725), 125; G. F. Nuttall, 'Early Quaker Letters from the Swarthmore MSS.' (typescript, FHL, 1952), 108.

69. *JGF*, i. 183; Nuttall, 'Early Quaker Letters', 135.

70. G. Fox and others, *Saul's Errand to Damascus* (1654), 30.

71. *Diary of the Rev. John Ward*, ed. C. Severn (1839), 141; Medical Society of London, 'Transcripts of John Ward's Diary 1648-1679', iv. 1119.

72. P. Gregg, *Free-born John* (1961), ch. 29; H. N. Brailsford, *The Levellers and the English Revolution* (1976), 637-40; J. Alsop,

'Gerrard Winstanley's Later Life', *P. and P.*, 82 (1979).

73.   C. Cheesman, *The Lamb Contending with the Lion* (1649).

74.   See K. Thomas, 'Another Digger Broadside', *P. and P.*, 42 (1969), 59, 65; *WTUD*, 99, n. 79; *JGF*, i. 194, ii. 32, 167, 169, 310; *FPT*, 6, 7; R. H. Evans, 'The Quakers of Leicestershire 1660-1714', *Transactions of the Leicestershire Archaeological Society*, xxviii (1952), map facing p. 63.

75.   Cf. E. E. Taylor, 'The First Publishers of Truth', *JFHS*, xix (1922); A. Cole, 'The Social Origins of the Early Friends', *JFHS*, xlviii (1957); R. T. Vann, 'Quakerism and the Social Structure in the Interregnum', *P. and P.*, 43 (1969); Vann, *Social Development*, 47-73; J. J. Hurwich, 'The Social Origins of the Early Quakers', *P. and P.*, 48 (1970); *MMB(1)*, xxvi-xxix; W. Spurrier, 'The Persecution of the Quakers in England: 1650-1714' (Univ. of North Carolina Ph.D. thesis, 1976), 225-55, 279-82; H. Forde, 'Derbyshire Quakers 1650-1761' (Univ. of Leicester Ph.D. thesis, 1977), ch. 3; *SQM*, 7; A. Anderson, 'The Social Origins of the Early Quakers', *QH*, lxviii (1979); B. Reay, 'The Social Origins of Early Quakerism', *Journal of Interdisciplinary History*, xi (1980).

76.   D. Cressy, *Literacy and the Social Order* (Cambridge, 1980), ch. 6.

77.   Cole, 'Social Origins', 117; Vann, 'Quakerism and the Social Structure', 72. For a further discussion of what follows – sources, problems etc. – see Reay, 'Social Origins'.

78.   R. H. Tawney, *The Agrarian Problem in the Sixteenth Century* (NY, 1967), 27-8. On the whole question of rank, see K. Wrightson, *English Society 1580-1680* (1982), ch. 1.

79.   PRO, E112/299/96; Essex RO, Q/R Th/1, fo. 17v; Essex RO, D/A BR 10/350; PRO, Prob 11/359/61.

80.   Cheshire RO, DLT/B27, pt 7; Cheshire RO, 'A new Freehold Book of Cheshire, 1671'; Somerset RO, DD/HI, Box 9 ('List of freeholders by hundreds'); and the lists of Cheshire and Somerset Quakers eligible as JPs in *Extracts*, 107, 110.

81.   PRO, Prob 11/325/166; Prob 11/444/52.

82.   FHL, Original Records of Sufferings MS. 610; Vann, *Social Development*, 14-15.

83.   Vann, 'The Social Origins of the Early Quakers: A Rejoinder', *P. and P.*, 48 (1970), 163; Vann, *Social Development*, 13.

84.   Anderson, 'Social Origins', 38.

85.   The Colchester 'gentlemen' were the John Furlys junior and senior, William Havens, and Thomas Bailes: merchant, draper, baymaker, and grocer respectively. They were also councillors during the Interregnum – Furly senior served several times as Mayor – so I have followed Vann in assuming that this would indicate gentry status.

86.   Hurwich, 'Social Origins', 159 (Warwickshire); Anderson, 'Social Origins', 38 (Lancashire).

87.   They were clearly marginal cases, described by the sources as both gents and yeomen. They were William Gandy of Over Whitley, and Randle Blackshaw junior, Hugh Strethill, and Richard Yerwood of Mobberley. For Blackshaw's father, see J. S. Morrill, *The Cheshire Grand Jury 1625-1659* (Leicester, 1976), 58.

88.   For the use of hearth tax returns, see Hurwich, 'Social Origins'; her 'Dissent and Catholicism in English Society: A Study of Warwickshire, 1660-1720', *Journal of British Studies*, xvi (1976); M. Spufford, 'The social status of some seventeenth-century rural Dissenters', *Studies in Church History*, viii (1972); Reay, 'Social Origins'. The problem with the hearth tax returns is that of regional variation. In the northern counties the average number of hearths is much lower, and returns do not reflect differences in wealth as clearly as, say, for Essex and Somerset. Although in Essex and Somerset a return of one hearth almost certainly guarantees that the occupant of the house was poor, the same is not true of Cheshire where several Cheshire yeomen of substance are listed under the one-hearth category. For this, see A. Macfarlane, *Reconstructing Historical Communities* (Cambridge, 1977), 162-3; Reay, 'Social Origins', Table 3.

89.   E. Pagitt, *Heresiography* (1654), 136; H. Hallywell, *An Account of Familism* (1673), 124.

90.   Hurwich, 'Social Origins', 159; Anderson, 'Social Origins', 38.

91.   Hurwich, 'Social Origins', 161.

92.   For a more detailed list of occupations, see Reay, 'Social Origins', Appendix 2.

93.   K. Wrightson and D. Levine, *Poverty and Piety in an English Village* (NY, 1979), 164, 166.

94.   Vann, *Social Development*, 81-2.

95.   G. Fox, *The Woman learning in Silence* (1656), 2.

96.   Fox, *Woman learning*, 1; K. Thomas, 'Women and the Civil War Sects', in T. Aston (ed.), *Crisis in Europe* (1970), 324-6.

97.   For Quaker women, see A. Lloyd, *Quaker Social History* (1950), ch. 8.

98.   York City Archives, Quarter Sessions Minute Book 1638-62, p. 353; R. Hubberthorne, *The Immediate Call* (1654); FHL, Swarthmore MS. i. 161; Vann, *Social Development*, 10; Cornwall RO, DD/SF 285, no. 64; *Extracts*, 20-21; *JGF*, ii. 461.

99.   M. M. Dunn, 'Saints and Sisters', *American Quarterly*, xxx (1980), 595-601. The figures for disruption of ministers are my own calculations from GBS, i, ii.

100.   Fox, *Woman learning*, 1.

101.   S. Fisher, *Rusticus Ad Academicos* (1660), pt iv, p. 3; J. G[askin], *A Just Defence* (1660), sig. A2v; T. Underhill, *Hell broke loose* (1660), 14.

102.   Braithwaite, *Beginnings*, 512; M. R. Watts, *The Dissenters* (Oxford, 1978), 270.

103.   See Reay, 'Early Quaker Activity', 55.

104.   Barbour, *Quakers*, 41-2, 58.

105.   Barbour, *Quakers*, 42, 55, 84, 86, 88-9.

106. Watts, *Dissenters*, 276, 285, 505-7, 509.

107. For my method of calculating the county populations of Quakers, see Reay, 'Early Quaker Activity', 55-6. The anti-tithe petition, *These Several Papers . . . sent to the Parliament* (1659), contains the names (county by county) of female Quakers, including children. The information on those arrested in 1661 is to be found in GBS, Besse, Somerset RO, DD/SFR 8/1, fols 3v-6, and [R. Wastfield and others], *For the King* [1661].

108. In calculating percentages of the county populations that were Quaker, I have followed the procedure of Watts: Reay, 'Early Quaker Activity', 59; Watts, *Dissenters*, 507.

109. The London estimations are based on W. Beck and T. F. Ball, *The London Friends' Meetings* (1869), 32; Warwickshire's on Hurwich, 'Dissent and Catholicism', 31; Wiltshire's on B. Williams, 'The Church of England and Protestant Nonconformity in Wiltshire 1645-1665' (Univ. of Bristol M. Litt. thesis, 1971), 222-3. Otherwise I have relied on the information provided in the sources mentioned in n. 107 above, and have followed the procedure outlined in Reay, 'Early Quaker Activity', 59, and Watts, *Dissenters*, 507.

110. My location of an extra pocket of Quakerism in the counties directly north and east of London corresponds with Watts's calculations for the early eighteenth century. He has found – using episcopal visitations and burial registers – that the Quakers were strongest in three areas: (1) Cumberland, Westmorland, and the Furness district of Lancashire; (2) Bristol; (3) London, Bedfordshire, Hertfordshire, Huntingdonshire, and Essex. See Watts, *Dissenters*, 276, 285, 505-7, 509.

111. The maps are based on data gathered from the sources listed in Reay, 'Social Origins', Appendix 1. Concentrations varied enormously within counties – from parishes where there were no Quakers whatsoever to places where nearly 20 per cent of the population were Friends.

2 EARLY QUAKERISM

1. H. R. Trevor-Roper, *Historical Essays* (1957), 224.

2. See R. T. Vann, 'From Radicalism to Quakerism: Gerrard

Winstanley and Friends', *JFHS*, xlix (1959), 45-6. The
conversion of the Leveller John Lilburne, usually cited to
support this sort of argument (e.g. M. R. Watts, *The Dissenters*
(Oxford, 1978), 207-8), is a bad example. Ironically, he was
one of the few Quakers to achieve an unequivocal pacifism
before 1660. And it is worth pointing out that Oliver Cromwell
was worried by Lilburne's conversion, thinking it a 'strange
politick contrivance', an attempt perhaps to enrol a party to
replace the Levellers? See *The Resurrection of John Lilburne*
(1656), 9; *Mercurius Politicus*, 379 (27 Aug.-3 Sept. 1657),
1597-8.

3. A. L. Morton, *The World of the Ranters* (1970), 18-19.

4. FHL, William Caton MS. iii. 147.

5. Cole, 'Quakers and the English Revolution', 348.

6. *WTUD*, 190.

7. *JGF*, ii. 149; W. P[enn], *The New Witnesses Proved Old
    Hereticks* (1672), 27, 33; S. Fisher, *Rusticus Ad Academicos*
    (1660), sig. B3. For Calvin, see *Concerning the Eternal
    Predestination of God* (1961) (translated by J. Reid), 58.

8. Fisher, *Rusticus Ad Academicos*, sig. B3; P. Cotton and M.
    Cole, *To the Priests* (1655), 1; G. Fox, *Newes Coming up out of
    the North* (1654), 3-17.

9. Cheshire RO, QJF 82/4/39; G. Fox and others, *Saul's Errand
    to Damascus* (1654), 10-11.

10. FHL, Swarthmore MS. iv. 22; *JFHS*, xvi (1919), 144.

11. Braithwaite, *Beginnings*, 147; *RDM*, 166.

12. See G. F. Nuttall, *The Holy Spirit in Puritan Faith and
    Experience* (Oxford, 1946).

13. See T. L. Underwood, 'Early Quaker Eschatology', in P. Toon
    (ed.), *Puritans, the Millennium and the Future of Israel* (1970),
    98.

14. *Records of the Churches of Christ*, ed. E. B. Underhill (1854),
    115.

15.   PRO, Assi 44/6; FHL, Swarthmore MS. iv. 52.

16.   G. F[ox], *A Declaration of the Difference* (1656), 12. George
       Keith, who led a schism in Pennsylvania in the 1690s, was to
       complain that large numbers of Quakers slighted the Bible: J.
       Butler, ' "Gospel Order Improved": The Keithian Schism and
       the Exercise of Quaker Ministerial Authority in Pennsylvania',
       William and Mary Quarterly, xxxi (1974), 434.

17.   *WTUD*, 214.

18.   Edward Burrough, quoted in Barbour, *Quakers*, 145.

19.   F. Howgil, *The Inheritance of Jacob* (1656), [21].

20.   Nuttall, *Holy Spirit*, 135.

21.   Underwood, 'Early Quaker Eschatology', 96.

22.   Isaac Penington, quoted in Underwood, 'Early Quaker
       Eschatology', 102.

23.   Barbour, *Quakers*, 187.

24.   T. L. Underwood, 'The Controversy Between the Baptists and
       Quakers in England 1650-1689' (Univ. of London Ph.D.
       thesis, 1965), 183; N. Smith, *The Quakers Spiritual Court*
       [1668], 1.

25.   FHL, William Caton MS. iii. 143-4; FHL, Swarthmore MS.
       iv. 83.

26.   J. Gilpin, *The Quakers Shaken* (Newcastle, 1653), 9; J.
       Toldervy, *The Foot out of the Snare* (1656), 35-7.

27.   *Quakers are Inchanters* (1655), 6.

28.   G. Emmot, *A Northern Blast or the Spiritual Quaker* (1655), 6.

29.   For going naked, see K. L. Carroll, 'Early Quakers and "Going
       Naked as a Sign" ', *QH*, lxvii (1978); and R. Bauman, *Let your
       words be few* (Cambridge, 1983), ch. 6. Richard Bauman
       argues that the ambiguity of the symbolism and the sheer shock
       value of going 'naked' obscured the intended message.
       Onlookers were so taken with the act that they did not recognize

its metaphorical significance. If they managed to look beyond the mere action, its symbolism was in any case ambiguous.

30.   Bristol RO, Orders of the Mayor and Aldermen 1653-1660, fol. 18v.

31.   G. F. Nuttall, *Studies in Christian Enthusiasm* (Wallingford, 1948), 35.

32.   *JGF*, ii. 428.

33.   FHL, Swarthmore MS. i. 373.

34.   FHL, Swarthmore MS. iv. 107, 108.

35.   *JGF*, ii. 154.

36.   G. F. Nuttall, *James Nayler: a Fresh Approach* (1954), 9; K. L. Carroll, 'Quaker Attitudes towards Signs and Wonders', *JFHS*, liv (1977), 74-6.

37.   R. F[arnworth], *Antichrists Man of War* (1655), 62.

38.   G. F. Nuttall, 'Unity with the creation: George Fox and the Hermetic Philosophy', *Friends' Quarterly*, i (1947).

39.   *Book of Miracles*, 22-3; FHL, Swarthmore MS. iii. 158.

40.   *Book of Miracles*, *passim*; *RDM*, 149; FHL, A. R. Barclay MS. 21.

41.   *Book of Miracles*, 14-15; *Diary of Ralph Josselin*, 367.

42.   *WTUD*, 193.

43.   See p. 32 above.

44.   *JGF*, i. 195.

45.   W. S[mith] and [E. Burrough], *The Reign of the Whore* (1659), 17.

46.   E. Burrough, *A Just and Lawful Tryal* (1660), 5; T. Ellwood, *The Foundation of Tythes Shaken* (1678), 446.

47. J. Braithwaite, *The Ministers of England* (1660), 12; M. Mason, *The Proud Pharisee Reproved* (1655), 39-40.

48. J. Fuce, *A Visitation* (1659), 2.

49. W. Tomlinson, *A Word of Reproof* (1656), 24; Cotton and Cole, *To the Priests*, 3, 6.

50. F. H[owgil], *The Great Case of Tythes* (1665), 55.

51. FHL, MS. Portfolio ix. 3; G. Bishop, *The Warnings of the Lord* (1660), 5ff.

52. [R. Farnworth], *A True Testimony* (1656), 8.

53. Burrough, *Just and Lawful Tryal*, 15.

54. For Quakers and elections, see Nottinghamshire RO, DD/SR 221/96/44 (I owe this reference to D. Hirst, *The Representative of the People?* (Cambridge, 1975), 14); FHL, Temp. MS. Box 98/1; J. S. Morrill, *Cheshire 1630-1660* (Oxford, 1974), 289; *Mercurius Politicus*, 324 (21-28 Aug. 1656), 7192.

55. For a more comprehensive treatment of the Quakers and the issue of tithes, see B. Reay, 'Quaker Opposition to Tithes 1652-1660', *P. and P.*, 86 (1980).

56. E. B[illing], *A Word of Reproof* (1659), 73; W. T[omlinson], *Seven Particulars* (1657), 21; J. Parnell, *The Trumpet of the Lord* (1655), 1.

57. FHL, MS. Portfolio iii. 5; Billing, *Word of Reproof*, 10, 77-8.

58. Billing, *Word of Reproof*, 20; FHL, MS. Portfolio iii. 5; E. B[illing?], *A Declaration of the Present Sufferings* (1659), 27-8; G. F[ox and P. M.], *An Instruction to Judges & Lawyers* (n.d.), 27-8.

59. B. Nicholson, *A blast from the Lord* (1653), 10.

60. G. F[ox], *A Declaration Against All Professions and Professors* (1655), 12; Nicholson, *A blast*, 10.

61. G. F[ox], *To the Parliament . . . Fifty nine Particulars* (1659), 8.

62.   M. Cranston, *John Locke* (1957), 281.

63.   FHL, A. R. Barclay MS. 167.

64.   G. Fox the younger, *A Noble Salutation* (1660), 5; *The Lambs Defence Against Lyes* (1656), 21.

65.   Fuce, *A Visitation*, 2.

66.   E. B[illing], *A Mite of Affection* (1659), *passim*.

67.   Quoted in Cole, 'Quakers and the English Revolution', 352.

68.   G. Fox the younger, *A Few Plain Words* (1659), 1-3.

69.   B. Reay, 'The Quakers and 1659: two newly discovered broadsides by Edward Burrough', *JFHS*, liv (1977), 110.

70.   Cole, 'Quakers and Politics', 15, 21, 35, 63-5, 276-7; Cole, 'Quakers and the English Revolution', 344-6.

71.   *JGF*, i. 161; G. F[ox], *To the Councill of Officers* (n.d.), 5.

72.   FHL, Swarthmore MS. vii. 157.

73.   *Resurrection of John Lilburne*, 10.

74.   J. Harwood, *To All People* (1663), 4.

75.   *Thurloe*, vi. 145-6; J. Price, *The Mystery and Method of his Majesty's Happy Restauration* (1680), 31.

76.   F. Howgil, *To all Commanders and Officers* (1657), 3 (not included in Howgil's works, *The Dawnings of the Gospel-Day* (1676)). Cf. also, E. Burrough [and G. Fox], *Good Counsel and Advice Rejected* (1659), 15; *To the Generals and Captains, Officers, and Souldiers, passim*; Fox, *To the Councill*, 5; FHL, Swarthmore MS. iv. 237.

77.   For Fox, see *JGF*, i. 334; for 1659, see ch. 5. below.

78.   J. C. [J. Collens or J. Crook?], *A Defence of the True Church* (1659), 29.

79.   Cole, 'Quakers and Politics', 20.

80.   FHL, MS. Portfolio i. 107.

81.   Bishop, *Warnings of the Lord*, 2-3.

82.   E. Burrough, *A Visitation & Warning Proclaimed* (1659), 35;
      Fox, *To the Councill*, 8; Burrough and Fox, *Good Counsel and
      Advice*, 36-7.

83.   *WTUD*, 194.

84.   Cole, 'Quakers and Politics', 284; Cole, 'Quakers and the
      English Revolution', 346.

85.   See B. Reay, 'Radicalism and Religion in the English
      Revolution', in J. F. McGregor and B. Reay (eds), *Radical
      Religion in the English Revolution* (Oxford, 1984), 16-17.

86.   Tomlinson, *Word of Reproof*, 6.

87.   PRO, E112/332/163, 206; E112/333/223, 248, 260, 274, 297.

88.   F. H[igginson], *A Brief Relation of the Irreligion of the
      Northern Quakers* (1653), 74.

89.   See Reay, 'Quaker Opposition to Tithes'.

90.   W. Albery, *A Millennium of Facts in the History of Horsham
      and Sussex* (Horsham, 1947), 415-16.

91.   PRO, Assi 44/5, Yorks. 1652.

92.   361 cases of disturbance of ministers (1654-9), listed in GBS, i,
      ii.

93.   As the Quaker James Parnell explained: 'amongst the great and
      rich ones of the Earth, they will either *thou* or *you* one another
      if they be equal in degree, as they call it; but if a man of low
      degree in the earth come to speak to any of them, then he must
      you the rich man, but the rich man will *thou* him'; 'if a poor man
      come before a rich man, it may be the rich man will move his
      hat, that is called courtesie and humility; but the poor man
      must stand with his hat off before him, and that is called honour
      and manners, and due respect unto him'. See J. Parnell, *A
      Shield of the Truth* (1655), 26-7.

94. Parnell, *Shield of the Truth*, 20-29; Billing, *Declaration of the Present Sufferings*, 27.

95. See C. Hill, 'Radical Prose in 17th Century England', *Essays in Criticism*, xxxii (1982); N. Smith (ed.), *A Collection of Ranter Writings* (1983).

96. R. Bauman, 'Aspects of 17th Century Quaker Rhetoric', *Quarterly Journal of Speech*, lvi (1970), 74.

97. George Fox, quoted by Bauman, '17th Century Quaker Rhetoric', 70. For Quaker plain language, see Bauman, *Let your words be few*, ch. 4.

98. Isaac Penington, quoted by Bauman, '17th Century Quaker Rhetoric', 67.

3 THE ELITE AND THE EARLY QUAKERS

1. *The Correspondence of John Locke*, ed. E. S. De Beer (Oxford, 1976), i. 41-2, 83-4, 126.

2. *Extracts*, 34.

3. C. M. Williams, 'An Unpublished Defence of the Quakers, 1655', *JFHS*, liv (1978).

4. *Letters of Early Friends*, ed. A. R. Barclay (1841), 37, 53-4, 59-60.

5. W. Stockdale and others, *The Doctrines and Principles of the Priests of Scotland* (1659), 2-3; W. Osbourne and others, *To You the Parliament sitting at Westminster* [1659].

6. Besse, i. 762, ii. 96; Nottinghamshire RO, DD/SR 211/96/4.

7. G. D. Langdon, *Pilgrim Colony* (New Haven, 1966), 69, 72-3, 75, 88; K. T. Erikson, *Wayward Puritans: A Study in the Sociology of Deviance* (NY, 1966), 107-36.

8. FHL, Swarthmore MS. i. 373; R. Farmer, *Sathan Inthron'd* (1657), 56; G. Whitehead, *The Christian Progress of that Ancient Servant* (1725), 125; *JGF*, i. 52, 110, 114-15, 181, 183, 189; FHL, Swarthmore MS. i. 179, iii. 80, 151, iv. 69, 141, 170.

9. For Ireland, see K. L. Carroll, 'Quakerism and the

Cromwellian Army in Ireland', *JFHS*, liv (1978).

10.   *A Journal of . . . William Edmundson* (1715), 28-9; FHL, A. R.
Barclay MS. 61; BL, Lansdowne MS. 821, fol. 68.

11.   See Reay, 'Early Quaker Activity', 59-62.

12.   Worcester College Library, Clarke MS. 48:2, 13, 27 March;
9, 15, 18, 20, 25, 29 May; 6, 16, 26, 27, 31 October; 2, 20, 21, 23
November 1657.

13.   Reay, 'Early Quaker Activity', 60-1, 63-4.

14.   *Thurloe*, iv. 508, vi. 168.

15.   Ibid, vi. 136.

16.   Reay, 'Early Quaker Activity', 61, 63.

17.   Cole, 'Quakers and the English Revolution', 342; R. Farmer,
The Impostor Dethron'd (1658), 43.

18.   PRO, Chester 24/131/2, 4; PRO, Chester 21/4, fol. 326; J. S.
Morrill, *Cheshire 1630-1660* (Oxford, 1974), 231.

19.   See Reay, 'Early Quaker Activity', 67.

20.   R. Howell, *Newcastle-upon-Tyne and the Puritan Revolution*
(Oxford, 1967), 258-61.

21.   Norfolk RO, Norwich QS Minute Book 1654-70, 1 January
1654/5.

22.   For example: F. H[owgil] and others, *Caines Bloudy Race*
(1657); Chester City RO, MF 75/11, 32, 66, 71; 76/42;
77(2)/55-7; Chester City RO, ML 3/375.

23.   A. D. Selleck, 'Plymouth Friends', *Devonshire Association*,
xcviii (1966), 292.

24.   M. V. Jones, 'The Political History of the Parliamentary
Boroughs of Kent, 1642-1662' (Univ. of London Ph.D. thesis,
1967), 473-5.

25.   East Sussex RO, SOF 5/1, pp. 7-8, 12-13, 24-5.

26.   Bristol RO, Orders of Mayor and Aldermen 1653-1660, fol. 26.

27.   *Essex Quarter Sessions Order Book, 1652-1661* (Chelmsford, 1974), 88; Cornwall RO, DD/SF 285/64; A. H. A. Hamilton, *Quarter Sessions from Queen Elizabeth to Queen Anne* (1878), 164-5; [G. Bishop], *The West Answering to the North* (1657), 69-70, 76-8, 107; Devon RO, QS Order Book 1652-1661, July 1656.

28.   Wiltshire RO, QS Great Rolls, Trinity 1656; *Somerset Assize Orders 1640-1659* (Somerset Rec. Soc., lxxi, 1971), 46-7.

29.   *Quarter Sessions Records of the County of Northampton* (Northants Rec. Soc., i, 1924), 155, 186; A. Audland and others, *The Saints Testimony* (1655), 2-3, 4, 8, 24.

30.   For disturbance of ministers (1654-9), see GBS, i, ii (listing over 350 instances, more than 300 of which were taken to the courts). For Cromwell's proclamation, *A Proclamation Prohibiting the Disturbing of Ministers* (1654).

31.   For example: R. Hubberthorne, *The Immediate Call* (1654); [J. Stubbs and W. Caton], *A True Declaration of the bloody Proceedings of the Men in Maidstone* (1655); East Sussex RO, QO/EW3, fol. 27v.

32.   M. Halhead and T. Salthouse, *The Wounds of an Enemie* (1656), 62.

33.   GBS, i. 344; Devon RO, QS Order Book 1652-1661, October 1657; Bodleian Library, MS Top. Oxon. F. 47, fol. 18v.

34.   *Extracts*, 14-20.

35.   PRO, Assi 44/5 Yorks. 1652.

36.   *Extracts*, 91.

37.   *Diary of Ralph Josselin*, 348, 367.

38.   For the Nayler episode, see Braithwaite, *Beginnings*, ch. 11; *A True Narrative of the Examination, Tryall . . . of James Nayler* (1657); T. Collier, *A Looking-Glasse for the Quakers* (1657), 16; W. Grigge, *The Quaker's Jesus* (1658); Worcester College Library, Clarke MS. 28, fols 120v-121, 122-122v, 123v, 125-

126; BL, Add. MS. 37682, fol. 59; *Correspondence of John Locke*, i. 43-4.

39.   *Diary of Thomas Burton*, i. 26-7, 67.

40.   *WTUD*, 201.

41.   *Diary of Thomas Burton*, i. 25, 96-8, 126; *The Devil turned Quaker* (1656), sig. A7.

42.   *Diary of Thomas Burton*, i. 33, 68-9, 78, 86, 97, 172-3.

43.   *Journals of the House of Commons*, vii. 468.

44.   J. Deacon, *An Exact History of the Life of James Naylor* [1657], 35-6.

45.   *Diary of Thomas Burton*, i. 49-50, 70, 110.

46.   *Journals of the House of Commons*, vii. 470.

47.   Bodleian Library, Rawlinson MS. A34, fol. 377.

48.   *Acts and Ordinances*, ii. 1098; *Diary of Thomas Burton*, i. 21-3, ii. 112-13.

49.   *Acts and Ordinances*, ii. 1162-70.

50.   Whitehead, *Christian Progress*, 133; GBS, i. 340, 341, 356-7; ii. Wilts., 3-4; Somerset RO, DD/SFR 8/1, pt i, fol. 31.

51.   GBS, i. 151, ii. Suffolk, 14; Essex RO, Q/SR 375/18; *Quarter Sessions Records of the County of Northampton*, 173.

52.   *Extracts*, 33, 47, 59; BL, Add. MS. 38856/74; GBS, i. 413, 414, 422; ii. Suffolk, 10, Yorks., 15, 16.

53.   Devon RO, QS Order Book 1652-1661, July and October 1658, January 1658/9.

54.   *Diary of Thomas Burton*, i. 137.

55.   Quoted by B. Easlea, *Witch Hunting, Magic and the New Philosophy* (Brighton, 1980), 221.

56. R. South, *Ecclesiastical Policy* (Oxford, 1660), 7; R. Sherlock, *The Quakers Wilde Questions* (1656), 217-18.

57. See L. Stone, *The Family, Sex and Marriage in England 1500-1800* (1977), ch. 5; G. J. Schochet, 'Patriarchalism, Politics and Mass Attitudes in Stuart England', *Historical Journal*, xii (1969), 420-1.

58. Stone, *Family, Sex and Marriage*, 152.

59. See P. Stubbes, *The Anatomie of Abuses* (1583), no pagination.

60. Barbour, *Quakers*, 164.

61. J. Parnell, *A Shield of the Truth* (1655), 26-7; Barbour, *Quakers*, 163-8.

62. J. Miller, *Antichrist in Man* (1655), 27.

63. Cornwall RO, DD/SF 285/64.

64. *The Cheshire Sheaf*, v (1970), 18.

65. *History of the Life of Thomas Ellwood* (1714), 47, 48, 57.

66. Quoted in *WTUD*, 198-9.

67. *Scotland and the Protectorate*, ed. C. Firth (Scottish Hist. Soc., xxxi, 1899), 362-3.

68. *Records of the Governor and Company of Massachusetts Bay* (Boston, 1853-4), iv, pt II, 165-6.

69. T. Philadelphus, *Exceptions Many and Just* (Oxford, 1653), 22; *Conway Letters*, ed. M. H. Nicolson (1930), 161.

70. [W. Fiennes], *Folly and Madnesse Made Manifest* (1659), 4.

71. See for example J. Clapham, *A Full Discovery* (1656).

72. R. Baxter, *One Sheet for the Ministry* (1657), 3.

73. See Bodleian Library, Rawlinson MS. D.376, fols. 187-8.

74. R. Clifton, 'The Popular Fear of Catholics during the English Revolution', *P. and P.*, 52 (1971), 33-4.

75. R. Baxter, *The Quakers Catechism* (1655), sig. C2.

76. W. Prynne, *A New Discovery of Some Romish Emissaries* (1656), 10; J. Noake, *Worcester Sects* (1861), 193: *The Publick Intelligencer*, 36 (2-9 June 1656), 605; *Mercurius Politicus*, 348 (5-12 Feb. 1656/7), 7587; Fiennes, *Folly and Madnesse*, 82-3; *The Correspondence of Bishop Brian Duppa and Sir Justinian Isham 1650-1660* (Northants. Rec. Soc., xvii, 1951), 186; J. Ives, *The Quakers Quaking* (1656), 43; J. Tombes, *True Old Light* (1660), sig. A2v; I. Bourne, *A defence of the Scriptures* (1656), sig. A2; *Conway Letters*, 306; *The Rev. Oliver Heywood . . . Autobiography*, ed. J. H. Turner (Brighouse, 1882-5), ii. 216.

77. G. F. Nuttall, *The Holy Spirit in Puritan Faith and Experience* (Oxford, 1946), 163-4; Baxter, *Quakers Catechism*, sig. C2v; Brownsword, *The Quaker-Jesuite* (1660); Prynne, *New Discovery*, 4; W. Prynne, *The Quakers Unmasked* (1664), 36-7; C. Fowler and S. Ford, *A Sober Answer* (1656), 16.

78. N. J. Smelser, *Theory of Collective Behaviour* (1962), 81, 85; H. Toch, *The Social Psychology of Social Movements* (NY, 1965), 52.

79. *Publick Intelligencer*, 36 (2-9 June 1656), 605.

80. Fiennes, *Folly and Madnesse*, 82-3; Miller, *Antichrist in Man*, 30ff; Baxter, *Quakers Catechism* [sig. C4].

81. P. Clark, *English Provincial Society . . . Kent, 1500-1640* (Hassocks, 1977), 394, 396.

4 POPULAR HOSTILITY TOWARDS QUAKERS

1. G. Whitehead, *The Christian Progress of that Ancient Servant* (1725), 12.

2. GBS, i. 2, 591-2; Friends' Meeting House, Kendal, MS. 51d, fol. 5; E. J. Evans, ' "Our Faithful Testimony": The Society of Friends and Tithe Payments, 1690-1730', *JFHS*, lii (1969), 109; FHL, MS. Wiltshire Quarterly Meeting Sufferings 1653-1702, p. 2; PRO, E112/299/140; E112/331/136; Somerset RO, DD/SFR 8/2, pt ii, fol. 31.

3. *FPT*, 125; Besse, i. 127; *Extracts*, 47, 59; Somerset RO, Q/SR, 98 pt 1/31.

4. M. Spufford, 'First steps in literacy', *Social History*, iv (1979), 431.

5. K. Wrightson, 'Two concepts of order', in J. Brewer and J. Styles (eds), *An Ungovernable People* (1980), ch. 1, esp. 21-2, 24, 29, 31, 44.

6. *FPT*, 33, 35, 36-7; *JGF*, i. 35-6, 41, 57-9, 60; FHL, A. R. Barclay MS. 14, 17; H. Smith, *Something further laid open* (1656), 1.

7. See chapter 5 below.

8. For example, *The Crowd in History* (1964), or *Paris and London in the Eighteenth Century* (1973).

9. A. Macfarlane, *Witchcraft in Tudor and Stuart England* (1970), chs 10-12.

10. *WTUD*, 188; e.g. *JGF*, i. 115.

11. E. B[illing], *A Word of Reproof* (1659), 11.

12. FHL, Swarthmore MS. i. 321; GBS, i. 422-4.

13. Besse, i. 87-8; Dorset RO, N10/A15, p. 3; FHL, MS. Portfolio, i. 73; Somerset RO, DD/SFR 8/1, pt i, fols 38, 38v; G. Fox the younger, *A True Relation* (1660), 3.

14. A. Fletcher, *A County Community in Peace and War: Sussex 1600-1660* (1975), 320.

15. A. Evans, *To the Most High and Mighty Prince Charles the II* (1660), 64.

16. *Mercurius Publicus*, 14 (3-10 April 1662), 230; 39 (25 Sept.-2 Oct. 1662), 643; 49 (29 Nov.-6 Dec. 1660), 792; *Kingdoms Intelligencer*, 32 (4-11 Aug. 1662), 529; F. Duke, *An Answer to some of the Principal Quakers* (1660), 67ff; J. D[auncy], *An Exact History* (1660), 201.

17. V. L. Ruland, 'A Royalist Account of Hugh Peter's Arrest',

Huntington Library Quarterly, xviii (1955), 178-82; C. E. Whiting, *Studies in English Puritanism* (1931), 556.

18.   W. I. Hull, *Benjamin Furly and Quakerism in Rotterdam* (Swarthmore, Penn., 1941), 237-8.

19.   *Leaves from the History of Welsh Nonconformity . . . Autobiography of Richard Davies*, ed. J. E. Southall (Newport, 1899), 68.

20.   Ibid, 12, 54-5.

21.   There is a mass of material. For some examples, see F. H[igginson], *A Brief Relation of the Irreligion of the Northern Quakers* (1653); J. Toldervy, *The Foot out of the Snare* (1656); J. Gilpin, *The Quakers Shaken* (Newcastle, 1653); G. Benson and others, *An Answer to John Gilpin's Book* (1655); *The Lambs Defence against Lyes* (1656); *Quakers are Inchanters* (1655); *Publick Intelligencer*, 31 (28 April-5 May 1656), 513-16; J. Clapham, *A Full Discovery* (1656); R. Blome, *The Fanatick History* (1660); W. Kennett, *A Register and Chronicle* (1728), 641; B. Capp, *Astrology and the Popular Press. English Almanacs 1500-1800* (1979), 234. I am grateful to Dr Margaret Spufford for the information on chapbooks.

22.   E.g. W. Prynne, *A New Discovery of Some Romish Emissaries* (1656), 10; R. Baxter, *The Quakers Catechism* (1655), sig. C2; *Publick Intelligencer*, 36 (2-9 June 1656), 605; *Mercurius Politicus*, 348 (5-12 Feb. 1656/7), 7587; J. Ives, *The Quakers Quaking* (1656), 43; J. Tombes, *True Old Light* (1660), sig. A2v; I. Bourne, *A defence of the Scriptures* (1656), sig. A2. For anti-Catholicism, see R. Clifton, 'The Popular Fear of Catholics during the English Revolution', *P. and P.*, 52 (1971); J. Miller, *Popery and Politics in England 1660-1688* (Cambridge, 1973), ch. 4.

23.   E.g. J. S[cotton], *Johannes Becoldus Redivivus: or the English Quaker, the German Enthusiast Revived* (1659).

24.   For prints and ballads, see *The Quakers Dream* (1655), frontispiece; *The Quakers Fear* (1656?), a ballad to be sung to the tune of 'Summer Time' or 'Bleeding Heart', reproduced on page 80 above; [Sir John Berkenhead], *The Four-Legg'd Quaker* (1659?), reproduced on page 48 above; Bodleian Library, Ashmole MS. 36, fols 88-9: 'Newes from Colchester, or a propper New Ballad of certaine carnall passages between a Quaker and a Colt'.

25.   *Leaves from the History of Welsh Nonconformity*, 54-5; FHL, Swarthmore MS. i. 315.

26.   [W. Addamson and others], *The Persecution of them people they call Quakers* [1656], 3; *Cain's Off-spring Demonstrated* (1659), 1; Dorset RO, N10/A15, p. 1; GBS, ii, Yorks., 17; FHL, A. R. Barclay MS. 17. See Besse, i. 254, 689, for other attacks upon outsiders.

27.   Clifton, 'Popular Fear of Catholics', 49; D. D. Bien, *The Calas Affair* (Princeton, 1960), 55, 146.

28.   See p. 94 below.

29.   P. Spufford, 'Population Mobility in Pre-Industrial England', *Genealogists Magazine*, xvii (1973-4); P. Clark, 'Migration in England during the late seventeenth and early eighteenth centuries', *P. and P.*, 83 (1979); P. Slack, 'Vagrants and Vagrancy in England, 1598-1664', *Economic History Review*, xxvii (1974).

30.   J. Cornwall, 'Evidence of Population Mobility in the Seventeenth Century', *Bulletin of the Institute of Historical Research*, xl (1967), 146, 150.

31.   K. Wrightson and D. Levine, *Poverty and Piety in an English Village* (NY, 1979), 76.

32.   Slack, 'Vagrants and Vagrancy' (the calculations of percentages are my own).

33.   P. Clark, 'The Migrant in Kentish Towns 1580-1640', in P. Clark and P. Slack (eds), *Crisis and Order in English Towns 1500-1700* (1972), 122, 127; Spufford, 'Population Mobility', 479.

34.   E. Skipp, *The Worlds Wonder* (1655), 11.

35.   'Swarthmore MS. Letters of John Audland', ed. C. Horle (typescript, FHL, 1975), no. 18. I am grateful to Mr Craig Horle for drawing my attention to this typescript.

36.   FHL, A. R. Barclay MS. 132.

37.   *The Journal . . . of Charles Marshall* (1844), 14-20.

38.   Clark, 'Migrant in Kentish Towns', 162, n. 105.

39.   R. Farmer, *The Great Mysteries of Godlinesse and
       Ungodlinesse* (1655), sigs A2, A2v.

40.   PRO, SP 18/97/87.

41.   East Sussex RO, SOF 5/1, pp. 1-4, 27-8; FHL, Swarthmore
       MS. i. 315.

42.   L. Koehler, *A Search for Power. The 'Weaker Sex' in
       Seventeenth-Century New England* (Urbana, 1980), 289; G.
       F[ox] and J. Rous, *To the Parliament of the Commonwealth of
       England* [*c.* 1659], 1-2.

43.   *Strange & Terrible Newes from Cambridge* (1659); J. Blackley
       and others, *A Lying Wonder Discovered* (1659); M. Spufford,
       Contrasting Communities (Cambridge, 1974), 285. John
       Bunyan was involved in the Cambridge accusations.

44.   Two Quaker witches were said to have confessed to having
       intercourse with the Devil. See Blome, *Fanatick History*, 117-
       18; [T. Smith], *A Gagg for the Quakers* (1659); PRO, Assi
       24/22, fol. 76.

45.   [W. Fiennes], *Folly and Madnesse Made Manifest* (1659), 4-5;
       J. Miller, *Antichrist in Man* (1655), 4; *The Devil turned Quaker*
       (1656), sig. A3.

46.   Cf. John Rule, 'Methodism, Popular Beliefs and Village
       Culture in Cornwall, 1800-50', in R. D. Storch (ed.), *Popular
       Culture and Custom in Nineteenth-Century England* (1982),
       63-6.

47.   *Biographical Dictionary of British Radicals in the Seventeenth
       Century*, ed. R. L. Greaves and R. Zaller (Brighton, 1982-4),
       i. 151; FHL, Swarthmore MS. i. 27; *JGF*, i. 169, 273; *Strange &
       Terrible Newes*, 7; A. N. Brayshaw, *The Personality of George
       Fox* (1933), 70; *Leaves from the History of Welsh
       Nonconformity*, 28, 36; Blome, *Fanatick History*, 114-15;
       Devil turned Quaker, [sig. A5]; T. Underhill, *Hell broke loose*
       (1660), 46; *Narrative Papers of George Fox*, ed. H. J. Cadbury
       (Richmond, Indiana, 1972), 22; GBS, i. 56; *The Diary of
       Samuel Pepys*, eds. R. Latham and W. Matthews (1971), iv.
       438; D. Roberts, *Memoirs of the Life of John Roberts* (1973), 48.

48. PRO, Assi 44/5, Yorks. 1652.

49. *Book of Miracles*, 95; *JGF*, i. 31-2, 38, 50, 104; Underhill, *Hell broke loose*, 48; Higginson, *Brief Relation*, 18-19; F. Bugg, *A Finishing Stroke* (1712), 240; *The Quaking Mountebanck* (1655), 17.

50. *Memoirs of the Life of John Roberts*, 56, 60.

51. *Quarter Sessions Records . . . for the County Palatine of Chester, 1559-1760* (Lancashire and Cheshire Rec. Soc., xciv, 1940), 164.

52. Brayshaw, *Personality of George Fox*, 27.

53. Higginson, *Brief Relation*, 18-19.

54. Higginson, *Brief Relation*, 11; PRO, Assi 44/5, Yorks. 1652.

55. L. Muggleton, *A Looking-Glass for George Fox* (1756), 46. In Salem, several decades later, this kind of behaviour was taken as symptomatic of witchcraft at work: P. Boyer and S. Nissenbaum, *Salem Possessed: The Social Origins of Witchcraft* (Cambridge, Mass., 1975), 4, 25-30.

56. Blome, *Fanatick History*, 117-18.

57. L. J. Ashford, *The History of the Borough of High Wycombe* (1960), 122.

58. For Quaker social origins, see ch. 1 above.

59. *Adventures by Sea of Edward Coxere*, ed. E. H. W. Meyerstein (Oxford, 1945), 99. See also *Narrative Papers of George Fox*, 23.

60. Besse, ii. 195.

61. See pp. 74-5 below.

62. The Mount School, York, MS. Friends' Letters: E. B[illing] to George Fox the Younger [1661]; *Adventures by Sea of Edward Coxere*, 86; *Cain's Off-Spring Demonstrated*, 1; GBS, ii, London, 3; Yorks., 17; Smith, *Something further laid open*, 1; *FPT*, 35; Dorset RO, N10/A15, p. 1; FHL, Swarthmore MS. i. 315, iv. 16, 314; Kent Archives Office, CP/BP 125; Besse, i.

87-8, 254; *The History of the Life of Thomas Ellwood* (1714), 78-9.

63. For attacks by students in Oxford and Cambridge, see Besse, i. 86-8, 565-6. And for pranksters, Besse, i. 566; some students 'proffer'd to put their Hands under Women's Aprons, and ask'd *If the Spirit were not there?*'

64. See C. Hill, *Change and Continuity in Seventeenth-Century England* (1974), ch. 8.

65. Rudé, *Crowd in History*, 224-5; Rudé, *Paris and London*, 289; N. Z. Davis, 'The Rites of Violence: Religious Riot in Sixteenth-Century France', *P. and P.*, 59 (1973), 54, 78-81. Though we should note her warning that for Catholic and Protestant popular violence in sixteenth-century France, 'the overall picture in these urban religious riots is not one of the "people" slaying the rich'. She suggests that socio-economic conflict was more likely in peasant risings.

66. Rudé, *Crowd in History*, 225.

67. *Life of Thomas Ellwood*, 78-9; FHL, Swarthmore MS. v. 93.

68. Essex RO, T/A 465/2, 21 June 1654, Nov. 1675.

69. A. B. Anderson, 'A Study in the Sociology of Religious Persecution: The First Quakers', *JRH*, ix (1977), 256.

70. See R. T. Vann, 'Quakerism and the Social Structure in the Interregnum', *P. and P.*, 43 (1969), 87; *MMB(1)*, xxviii; B. Reay, 'The Social Origins of Early Quakerism', *Journal of Interdisciplinary History*, xi (1980), 69-72.

71. For hostility to middlemen, see R. B. Westerfield, *Middlemen in English Business* (Yale, 1915), 126-7; E. P. Thompson, 'The Moral Economy of the English Crowd', *P. and P.*, 50 (1971); J. Walter and K. Wrightson, 'Dearth and the Social Order in Early Modern England', *P. and P.*, 71 (1976).

72. Hertfordshire RO, QSMB 4/41; *Bedfordshire County Records . . . Sessions Minute Books 1651 to 1660* (Bedford, n.d.), 14; Essex RO, Q/SR 396/9, 397/14; Essex RO, T/A 465/34, 1654/5.

73. Hertfordshire RO, QSMB 3/377, 388; Essex RO, T/A 465/2, Nov. 1675.

74. Thompson, 'Moral Economy', 95, n. 62; Braithwaite, *Second Period*, 564, n. 4; A. Charlesworth, *An Atlas of Rural Protest in Britain 1548-1900* (1983), 111.

75. J. Stevenson, *Popular Disturbances in England 1700-1870* (1979), 30.

76. See V. Bailey, 'Salvation Army Riots, the "Skeleton Army" and Legal Authority in the Provincial Town', in A. P. Donajgrodzki (ed.), *Social Control in Nineteenth Century Britain* (1977).

77. S. Wilde, *The Last Legacy* (1703), 2.

78. BL, Add. MS. 29624, pp. 377-9; GBS, ii, London, 3; *Life of Thomas Ellwood*, 78-9; Braithwaite, *Beginnings*, 474; Besse, i. 87-8, 742.

79. GBS, ii, London, 3.

80. My account of the riots is based on J. Latimer, *The Annals of Bristol in the Seventeenth Century* (Bristol, 1900), 256-7; G. Bishop and others, *The Cry of Blood and Herod* (1656), 14-15, 16, 27-31; G. Bishop, *The Throne of Truth Exalted* (1657), 57; W. Sewel, *The History of the Rise, Increase, and Progress of . . . Quakers* (1722), 84-5; Bristol RO, Orders of Mayor and Aldermen 1653-1660, fol. 12v.

81. *A Letter of the Apprentices of the City of Bristol* (1660); Bristol RO, Common Council Proceedings 1659-1675, p. 12; FHL, Swarthmore MS. iv. 134.

82. D. V. Glass, 'Socio-economic Status and Occupations in the City of London at the End of the Seventeenth Century', in A. E. J. Hollaender and W. Kellaway (eds), *Studies in London History* (1969), 387-8; S. R. Smith, 'The Social and Geographical Origins of the London Apprentices, 1630-1660', *Guildhall Miscellany*, iv (1973). For Rudé, see *Crowd in History*, 205, 207; *Paris and London*, 299.

83. See *Merchants and Merchandise in Seventeenth-Century Bristol* (Bristol Rec. Soc., xiv, 1955), 276-7.

84. See S. R. Smith, 'The London Apprentices as Seventeenth-Century Adolescents', *P. and P.*, 61 (1973), 157, 161; B. Capp, 'English Youth Groups', *P. and P.*, 76 (1977), 127-33; Davis, 'Rites of Violence', 87-8; N. Z. Davis, 'The Reasons of Misrule: Youth Groups and Charivaris in Sixteenth-Century France', *P. and P.*, 50 (1971); B. Scribner, 'Reformation, carnival and the world turned upside-down', *Social History*, iii (1978).

85. Davis, 'Rites of Violence', 87-8.

86. Smith, 'London Apprentices as Seventeenth-Century Adolescents', 161.

87. In a curious episode in the parish of Peasmarsh in Sussex in 1657 a Quaker was invited to a house by two youths and some young women. He was overpowered by the men, his trousers were lowered, and he was beaten by the women – with a three-foot rod. Quite probably I am reading too much into the affair, but is it possible that he was being punished for stepping outside the bounds of community convention by turning Quaker? The punishment does appear somewhat ritualistic, and it seems significant that the Quaker was beaten by women and not the youths who retired discreetly. It is also interesting that the episode had respectable sanctions: it was said to have been organized by a 'Rich man of the Towne'. See East Sussex RO, SOF 5/1, p. 19.

88. E. P. Thompson, *The Making of the English Working Class* (1968), 74, 79-80. For other examples, see R. B. Rose, 'The Priestly Riots of 1791', *P. and P.*, 18 (1960); J. Walsh, 'Methodism and the mob in the eighteenth century', *Studies in Church History*, viii (1972), 216-18; Bailey, 'Salvation Army Riots', 243ff.

89. Besse, i. 87-8; East Sussex RO, SOF 5/1, pp. 27-8; and pp. 93, 95, 96, 99 below.

90. T. Morford, *The Cry of Oppression* (1659), 18-19.

91. Bristol RO, Orders of Mayor and Aldermen 1653-1700, fol. 12v; Bishop, *Cry of Blood*, 29-31.

92. *Record of the Sufferings of Quakers in Cornwall 1655-1686*, ed. N. Penney (1928), 23-4; Besse, i. 115-16.

93.   Kent Archives Office, CP/BP 125.

94.   FHL, Swarthmore MS. iv. 16.

95.   For Jacobins, see Thompson, *Making of the English Working Class*, 122-3.

96.   For Clubmen, see D. Underdown, *Somerset in the Civil War and Interregnum* (1973), 133; J. S. Morrill, *The Revolt of the Provinces* (1976), 98-111, 196-200.

97.   See Davis, 'Rites of Violence', 66-9.

98.   FHL, A. R. Barclay MS. 14, 17. Priests led attacks on Quaker meetings in Liverpool and Somerset: GBS, i. 561; FHL, Swarthmore MS. iii. 163.

99.   FHL, Swarthmore MS. i. 315.

100.   Dorset RO, N10/A15, p. 1.

101.   Hostility towards Quakers in the seventeenth century is strikingly similar to hostility towards Methodists in the eighteenth: see Walsh, 'Methodism and the mob', 213-27 (the quotations come from pp. 222, 223). I am grateful to Mr Keith Thomas for drawing my attention to this article.

102.   For examples of sectarian ties cutting across families, see *Sufferings of Quakers in Cornwall*, 17ff; Somerset RO, DD/SFR 8/1, pt i, fol. 26v; *Life of Thomas Ellwood*, 47ff. For fears of the effect of Quakers upon the family, see G. Fox and others, *Saul's Errand to Damascus* (1654), 1; G. Emmot, *A Northern Blast or the Spiritual Quaker* (1655), 6; Higginson, *Brief Relation*, 75; Farmer, *Great Mysteries of Godlinesse and Ungodlinesse*, 87; *The Querers and Quakers Cause* (1653), 14-15; *The Quakers terrible Vision* (1655), 5.

103.   FHL, Swarthmore MS. vi. 51.

104.   PRO, Assi 44/5, Yorks. 1652.

105.   Davis, 'Rites of Violence', 61-5.

106.   E.g. G. F[ox], *To Those that have been formerly in Authority* [1660], 5.

107.   Morrill, *Revolt of the Provinces*, 110.

5 THE QUAKERS, 1659, AND THE RESTORATION OF MONARCHY

1.   G. Davies, *The Restoration of Charles II 1658-1660* (Oxford,
           1969); A. H. Woolrych, 'The Good Old Cause and the Fall of
           the Protectorate', *Historical Journal*, xiii (1957); *idem*, 'Last
           Quests for a Settlement 1657-1660', in G. E. Aylmer (ed.), *The
           Interregnum* (1972), ch. 8; *idem*, 'Introduction', in *Complete
           Prose Works of John Milton: VII (1659-1660)* (New Haven,
           1980), 4-228.

2.   Capp, *Fifth Monarchy Men*, 130; C. Hill, *The Century of
           Revolution 1603-1714* (1980), 120-1.

3.   See T. Barnard, *The English Republic 1649-1660* (Harlow,
           1982), ch. 8: 'Epilogue: Towards the Restoration of Charles
           II'. Note also the end date in the title of Derek Hirst's new
           book: *Authority and Conflict. England 1603-1658* (1984).

4.   *Diary of Ralph Josselin*, 457-8.

5.   D. White, *A Diligent Search* (1659), 4; G. F[ox], *The Lambs
           Officer* (1659), 1, 13 (a copy in the Bodleian Library (C. 13.6
           Linc.) is bound with tracts printed during the restoration of
           the Rump in May, so we can assume that it appeared in that
           month).

6.   E. Burrough, *To the Parliament of the Common-Wealth of
           England* (1659) (12 Sept.).

7.   F. Howgil, *An Information and also Advice* (1659), 5.

8.   E. Burrough, *To the Whole English Army* (1659). This
           pamphlet was omitted from his collected works, *The
           Memorable Works of a Son of Thunder* (1672).

9.   E. Burrough, *To the Parliament of the Common-Wealth of
           England* (1659) (6 Oct.), 3. This radical tract was not included
           in Burrough's works.

10.   R. H[ubberthorne], *The Good Old Cause* (1659), [7]; see also
           G. Bishop, *Mene Tekel* (1659), 4.

11.   H. Smith and others, *The Fruits of Unrighteousnes* (1658), 13.

12.   E. B[urrough], *Satans Designe Defeated* (1659), 19.

13.   *The Copie of a Paper presented to the Parliament* (1659); *These Several Papers . . . Sent to the Parliament* (1659); GBS, i. 138; Friends' Meeting House, Kendal, MS. 103, fol. 9.

14.   *WTUD*, 196; J. Crook, *Tythes No Property* (1659), sig. A2v.

15.   G. Bishop, *The Warnings of the Lord* (1660), 19; G. F[ox], *To the Parliament . . . Fifty nine Particulars* (1659), 4-5; E. B[illing], *A Mite of Affection* (1659), 2-3, 5; G. Fox, *Several Papers Given Forth* (1660), 32-3.

16.   Cole, 'Quakers and Politics', 277.

17.   J. Crook and others, *A Declaration of the People of God* (1659), 5.

18.   *Extracts*, 6-13, 105-15.

19.   See B. Reay, 'The Quakers and 1659: two newly discovered broadsides by Edward Burrough', *JFHS*, liv (1977).

20.   Dr Williams's Library, MS. 59, vi, fol. 235v. See also W. Prynne, *A true and perfect Narrative* (1659), 20, quoted in Underdown, *Pride's Purge*, 349; *CSP, 1659-60*, 5; Worcester College Library, Clarke MS. 31, fols 164-164v; R. Baxter, *Right Rejoycing* (1660), 47.

21.   *The Nicholas Papers* (Camden Third Series, xxxi, 1920), 151-2; *Thurloe*, vii. 704.

22.   M. Guizot, *History of Richard Cromwell and the Restoration of Charles II* (1856), i. 407-8.

23.   *HMC: Report on the Manuscripts of F. W. Leyborne-Popham* (1899), 141.

24.   Guizot, *Richard Cromwell*, i. 453; *The Londoners Last Warning* (n.d.), 4 (a MS. note in the Bodleian copy, Wood 610 (11), dates it Aug. 1659); Clarendon MS. 63, fol. 263.

25.   *Diary of Sir Archibald Johnston of Wariston* (Scottish Hist. Soc., xxxiv, 1940), 133.

26.   *The Letters and Journals of Robert Baillie*, ed. D. Laing
        (Edinburgh, 1842), iii. 429.

27.   Clarendon MS. 61, fols 205, 325; Guizot, *Richard Cromwell*,
        i. 458, ii. 268, 304; *A Brief Account . . . of the Committee of
        Safety* (1659), 19; *Diary of Sir Archibald Johnston*, 139; Dr
        Williams's Library, MS. 59, iv, fol. 281. For Vane and the
        Quakers, see V. A. Rowe, *Sir Henry Vane the Younger* (1970),
        223-4; Cole, 'Quakers and Politics', 156-7, 160, 193. Vane had
        estates in Durham at Raby Castle and Barnard Castle; both
        were Quaker areas. The Quaker connection continued after
        Vane's execution. Lady Vane's steward at Raby was sympathetic
        to the sect, while Vane's son Christopher got Quaker support
        as a Whig candidate in the election of 1679; M. S. Child, 'Prelude
        to Revolution: The Structure of Politics in County Durham,
        1678-88' (Univ. of Maryland Ph.D. thesis, 1972), 298, n. 157,
        305.

28.   M. Cranston, *John Locke* (1957), 43.

29.   *A Collection of Original Letters and Papers*, ed. T. Carte
        (1739), ii. 225; *Weekly Intelligencer*, 25 (18-25 Oct. 1659), 199.

30.   Guizot, *Richard Cromwell*, ii. 284; J. Nicoll, *A Diary of Public
        Transactions* (Edinburgh, 1836), 257; *The Letter Book of John
        Viscount Mordaunt* (Camden Third Series, lxix, 1945), 80; M.
        James, 'The Political Importance of the Tithes Controversy in
        the English Revolution', *History*, xxvi (1941), 18.

31.   A. H. Woolrych, 'Politics and Political Theory in England
        1658-1660' (Univ. of Oxford B. Litt. thesis, 1952), 79-80. For
        the Rump's earlier life, see B. Worden, *The Rump Parliament
        1648-1653* (Cambridge, 1974).

32.   See FHL, Swarthmore MS. i. 145; *Journals of the House of
        Commons*, vii. 648; *Faithful Scout*, 5 (20-27 May 1659), 38-9;
        R. Hubberthorne, *A Word of Wisdom* (1659). For the release of
        Quakers, see GBS, i. 149, 150, 162, 435, 455, 506, 591; ii,
        Somerset, 1-4, 45-6; iv. 501; *The Northern Queries* [1659], 5.

33.   Bishop, *Warnings*, 35.

34.   *Journals of the House of Commons*, vii. 647; [J. Taylor], *A
        Loving & Friendly Invitation* (1683), 13. The lists are in PRO,
        SP 18/102/50, SP 18/203/8-9, 13, 18, 21-8, and are printed in

Extracts, 6-13, 105-15. Quaker complaints against William Boteler for 'dealing unjustly' with the Quaker William Lovell were used in the House of Commons in June to prevent Boteler's appointment as a colonel of horse: see Davies, *Restoration*, 108; *Extracts*, 8.

35.   J. S. Morrill, *Cheshire 1630-1660* (Oxford, 1974), 258-9. Dr Morrill was obviously unaware that they are Quaker lists.

36.   *Journals of the House of Commons*, vii. 662; Carte, *Collection*, ii. 225; *Publick Intelligencer*, 198 (10-17 Oct. 1659), 783; *Weekly Post*, 9 (28 June-5 July 1659), 77. The Quaker position is best described by George Bishop in his criticism of the Army's declaration of 12 May 1659: *Mene Tekel*, 14ff.

37.   *Journals of the House of Commons*, vii. 683, 694; *Copie of a Paper*.

38.   Guizot, *Richard Cromwell*, i. 424-5.

39.   D. Veall, *The Popular Movement for Law Reform 1640-1660* (Oxford, 1970), 96; *Memoirs of Edmund Ludlow*, ed. C. H. Firth (Oxford, 1894), ii. 133.

40.   Davies, *Restoration*, 157-8; *Memoirs of Edmund Ludlow*, ii. 161-2, 169; Dr Williams's Library, MS. 59, iv, fol. 274v.

41.   FHL, William Caton MS. iii. 400-3.

42.   Worcester College Library, Clarke MS. 32, fols 172v-173; *Memoirs of Edmund Ludlow*, ii. 169.

43.   *JGF*, i. 334-5.

44.   See *Diary of Sir Archibald Johnston*, 129-30.

45.   See H. Denne, *The Quaker No Papist* (1659); *Memoirs of Edmund Ludlow*, i., pp. xxviii, xxix; B[illing], *Mite of Affection*; W. Sprigge, *A Modest Plea for an Equal Commonwealth* (1659); H. Stubbe, *An Essay in Defence of the Good Old Cause* (1659); J. Canne and J. Osborne, *A Indictment Against Tythes* (1659).

46.   Capp, *Fifth Monarchy Men*, 124; BL, Stowe MS. 189, fol. 64; *Copie of a Paper*, title page; Denne, *Quaker No Papist*; H.

Stubbe, *A Light Shining out of Darknes* (1659), 81-92 (see also his *Malice Rebuked* (1659), 36); E. Lewis Evans, 'Morgan Llwyd and the Early Friends', *Friends' Quarterly*, viii (1954), 57; S. Duncon, *Several Proposals* (1659), postscript.

47.   Edward Earl of Clarendon, *The History of the Rebellion and Civil Wars in England* (Oxford, 1969), vi. 176.

48.   *A Letter from Sir George Booth* (Chester, 1659).

49.   Stubbe, *An Essay*, preface.

50.   See Bodleian Library, Rawlinson MS. C179, pp. 173-4; *CSP, 1659-60*, 219; *An Alarum to Corporations* (1659).

51.   D. Underdown, *Somerset in the Civil War and Interregnum* (1973), 190.

52.   That Cheshire confirms to the sectarian image makes sense in the light of Booth's allegations. The Cheshire commissioners included an ally of the Quakers, John Bradshaw, six men recommended by the Quakers (in May) as being 'moderate' – a good gauge of radicalism – and one Quaker. Two Quakers were named in the Berkshire list, along with three moderate men and only one whom the Quakers had considered a persecutor; the list also included Henry Marten, Cornelius Holland, and George Joyce. See Morrill, *Cheshire*, 231, 258-9, 289, 298; *Extracts*, 105, 110; *Acts and Ordinances*, 1320, 1321.

53.   A. Fletcher, *A County Community in Peace and War: Sussex 1600-1660* (1975), 317.

54.   L. F. Brown, *The Political Activities of the Baptists and Fifth Monarchy Men* (Washington, 1912), 185; Capp, *Fifth Monarchy Men*, 124.

55.   *Acts and Ordinances*, 1290; [R. Rich], *Hidden Things brought to Light*, (1678), 29.

56.   *Acts and Ordinances*, 1320, 1321, 1322, 1325, 1327, 1328, 1333, 1334, 1335. For identification of the Quakers, see *Extracts*, 105, 110, 111; *JGF*, i. 225, 237, 259, 262, 444; *FPT*, 282-3, 324, 370; Besse, i. 744. Professor Cole includes Robert Duncon in the Suffolk list (Cole, 'Quakers and the English Revolution', 351, n. 46), but he may well have been the

Quaker's uncle of the same name: G. Whitehead, *The Christian Progress of that Ancient Servant* (1725), 135; G. F. Nuttall, *Visible Saints* (Oxford, 1957), 150, n. 3. For Munckton, see K. Lindley, *Fenland Riots and the English Revolution* (1982), 196.

57. *Acts and Ordinances*, 1332; FHL, Swarthmore MS. iii. 143, vii. 157; Clarendon MS. 63, fol. 208.

58. *Acts and Ordinances*, 1335; T. Lewis and others, *For the King and both Houses of Parliament* [1661], 5; *Leaves from the History of Welsh Nonconformity . . . Autobiography of Richard Davies*, ed. J. E. Southall (Newport, 1899), 56-7, 62.

59. FHL, A. R. Barclay MS. 169; PRO, SP 29/45/42, 60; SP 29/49/27; *Journals of the House of Commons*, vii. 753; BL, Add. MS. 21425, fol. 124; GBS, ii, Yorks., 26; Humberside RO, DD QR/24: 'In the year 1665'; *HMC Leyborne-Popham*, 156-7; *Mercurius Publicus*, 4 (24-31 Jan. 1660/1), 62-3; Chester City RO, MF/88, 5 June 1670; FHL, Swarthmore MS. iii. 146.

60. FHL, Swarthmore MS. iii. 145.

61. Haggatt was a long-time associate of the Bristol Quakers Hollister and Bishop, and his wife was a Quaker. Colonel William West, another with Quaker contacts, was generally sympathetic to the sect (*JGF*, index: William West). Bradshaw treated the Quakers very leniently on the Cheshire assize circuit, and also received support from them in parliamentary elections (Morrill, *Cheshire*, 231, 289, 298). Southwark was a Quaker area, and Vane (see n. 27 above) had many Quaker contacts. The sect also seems to have been favourably disposed towards Rainborough (*Extracts*, 7). For the raising of these regiments, see *Journals of the House of Commons*, vii. 749, 753; Bodleian Library, Rawlinson MS. C179, p.209; *Mercurius Politicus*, 582 (4-11 Aug. 1659), 656.

62. Underdown, *Somerset*, 186, 190; *Extracts*, 107; J. Whiting, *Persecution Expos'd*, 130 (for Anderdon).

63. Bodleian Library, Rawlinson MS. C179, p. 245 (for Mansell's appointment); F. Gawler, *A Record of Some Persecutions* (1659), 7, 17, 18, 25 (for Quaker soldiers in Wales); FHL, Swarthmore MS. iv. 219.

64. Capp, *Fifth Monarchy Men*, 124; Brown, *Political Activities of the Baptists*, 185.

65. G. W[hitehead], *Christ's Lambs Defended* (1691), 27; W. Sewel, *The History of the Rise, Increase, and Progress of . . . Quakers* (1722), 211; *JGF*, i. 334.

66. *CSP, 1658-9*, 387; *CSP, 1659-60*, 240; *Journals of the House of Commons*, vii. 817; *HMC Leyborne-Popham*, 168-9. Both Edward Billing and Richard Hubberthorne seem to have known Rich. According to Hubberthorne, Rich attended a Quaker meeting in London in May 1660. FHL, Swarthmore MS. iv. 18, v. 93.

67. FHL, A. R. Barclay MS. 17; *Thurloe*, vi. 635; FHL, Swarthmore MS. iv. 237; Worcester College Library, Clarke MS. 48, 26 Oct., 31 Oct., 2 Nov., 23 Nov. 1657; A. D. Selleck, 'Plymouth Friends', *Devonshire Association*, xcviii (1966), 298.

68. *Thurloe*, vi. 136; Worcester College Library, Clarke MS. 48, 9 May, 29 May 1657; *JGF*, i. 303; FHL, Swarthmore MS. iv. 217; FHL, William Caton MS. iii. 401; PRO, SP 29/22/118 (for Ashfield's claim that he was not a Quaker).

69. J. Hodgson, *A Letter from a Member of the Army* (1659). See A. Cole, 'The Peace Testimony in 1659', *JFHS*, xlvi (1954), 48-52.

70. FHL, Luke Howard MS. 8.

71. A. H. Dodd, *Studies in Stuart Wales* (Cardiff, 1971), 113-14, 163; Lewis and others, *For the King*, 5, 6; *Journals of the House of Commons*, vii. 740; *JGF*, i. 262, 446.

72. *Journals of the House of Commons*, vii. 669, 679; Sir J. Berry and S. G. Lee, *A Cromwellian Major General* (Oxford, 1938), 170, 228; Worcester College Library, Clarke MS. 48, 16 Oct., 27 Oct. 1657; The Mount School, York, MS. Friends' Letters: E. Billing to G. Fox the younger [1661].

73. Davies, *Restoration*, 107. For Tomlinson (the Quaker), see my entry in the *Biographical Dictionary of British Radicals in the Seventeenth Century*, ed. R. L. Greaves and R. Zaller (3 vols, Hassocks, 1983-4).

74. FHL, MS. Portfolio i. 107.

75. FHL, Luke Howard MS. 8.

76. FHL, Swarthmore MS. iv. 268, 279.

77. F. Howgil, *The Popish Inquisition* (1659), 68.

78. R. Farmer, *The Impostor Dethron'd* (1658), 39.

79. GBS, iii. 695; T. M[orford], *Deceit and Enmity* (1659), [2]; W. Stockdale and others, *The Doctrines and Principles of the Priests of Scotland* (1659), 18, 59, 72.

80. GBS, i. 155.

81. Smith, *Fruits of Unrighteousnes*, 28.

82. J. C[ollens], *A Word in Season* (1660), 7.

83. Smith, *Fruits of Unrighteousnes*, 28; GBS, i. 153.

84. Fox, *Several Papers*, 43.

85. Farmer, *Impostor Dethron'd*, 115.

86. T. Danson, *The Quakers Wisdom* (1659), 'a narrative', 1-6; S. Fisher, *Rusticus Ad Academicos* (1660), part i, 32-4; R. Blome, *The Fanatick History* (1660), 119-21.

87. R. South, *Interest Deposed* (Oxford, 1660), 19. See J. S[cotton], *Johannes Becoldus Redivivus: or the English Quaker, the German Enthusiast Revived* (1659).

88. Prynne, *True and perfect Narrative*, 88.

89. F. H[owgil], *One of Antichrist's Voluntiers Defeated* (1660), 30; Bodleian Library, Rawlinson MS. C179, pp. 30-1.

90. *Mercurius Politicus*, 580 (21-28 July 1659), 617-18.

91. M. Spufford, *Contrasting Communities* (Cambridge, 1974), 285, 290; J. Blackley and others, *A Lying Wonder Discovered* (1659); *Loyall Scout* (22-29 July 1659), 106; F. B. Tolles, 'A Quaker's Curse', *Huntington Library Quarterly*, xiv (1950-1), 415-21; *Weekly Intelligencer*, 12 (19-26 July 1659), 96. Many of the stories were collected by Blome, *Fanatick History* (1660), 109-21, but they had been circulating in 1659.

92. GBS, ii, London, 3-4; iii. 694-5; i. 138; Bodleian Library, Rawlinson MS. C179, pp. 24, 30-1.

93. Somerset RO, DD/SFR 8/1, pt i, fols 31v, 37v; Dorset RO, N10/A15, p. 1; *Quarter Sessions Records for the County of Somerset* (Somerset Rec. Soc., xxviii, 1912), 370-1.

94. GBS, iii. 659.

95. R. Berd and others, *To the Parliament* (1659), 2.

96. *Record of the Sufferings of Quakers in Cornwall 1655-1686*, ed. N. Penney (1928), 23-4; Besse, i. 115-16.

97. Edward Earl of Clarendon, *State Papers* (Oxford, 1767-1786), iii. 489-90.

98. Morrill, *Cheshire*, 318-19; *Letter from Sir George Booth*.

99. *Publick Intelligencer*, 188 (1-8 Aug. 1659), 640; H. Stubbe, *A Letter to An Officer* (1659), 10; F. Howgil, *The Mouth of the Pit Stopped* (1659), 15-16.

100. Morrill, *Cheshire*, 313-15, 322-3; *Weekly Intelligencer*, 16 (16-23 Aug. 1659), 123; *The Autobiography of Henry Newcome* (Chetham Soc., xxvi, 1852), i. 109; PRO, SP 23/243/168; *The Life of Adam Martindale* (Chetham Soc., iv, 1845), 137; Clarendon MS. 64, fol. 339v.

101. *The Life and Times of Anthony Wood*, ed. A. Clark (Oxford, 1891), i. 280-1.

102. *Mercurius Politicus*, 580 (21-28 July 1659), 617-18; 584 (18-25 Aug. 1659), 681; *Publick Intelligencer*, 187 (25 July-1 Aug. 1659), 617; 190 (15-22 Aug. 1659), 668.

103. Spufford, *Contrasting Communities*, 290, n. 75; Blackley, *Lying Wonder*.

104. Berd, *To the Parliament*, 2-4.

105. *Mercurius Politicus*, 58[?] (24 Aug.-1 Sept. 1659), 692.

106. BL, Add. MS. 32324, fol. 43.

107. Clarendon MS. 64, fols 153, 264, 266.

108. PRO, SP 23/263/36.

109. Clarendon MS. 64, fols 190-190v.

110. *Diaries and Letters of Philip Henry*, ed. M. H. Lee (1882), 69.

111. [T. Smith], *A Gagg for the Quakers* (1659), [2].

112. [W. Fiennes], *Folly and Madnesse Made Manifest* (1659), 7.

113. R. B[lome], *Questions Propounded to George Whitehead* (1659), 7; Fiennes, *Folly and Madnesse*, 2, 18-20.

114. T. Underhill, *Hell broke loose* (1660), 5-10. The tract is wrongly dated: it appeared in November 1659: Howgil, *Mouth of the Pit*, 6.

115. H. Bache, *The Voice of Thunder* (1659), 1.

116. *Cain's Off-spring Demonstrated* (1659).

117. Guizot, *Richard Cromwell*, i. 403.

118. E. Reynolds, *The Brand Pluck'd out of the Fire* (1659), 32, 36; E. Reynolds, *The Misery of a Deserted People* (1659), 28; E. Reynolds and others, *A Seasonable Exhortation* (1660), 4, 6 (it had been intended to publish the tract in 1659).

119. J. S., *The Jesuite Discovered* (1659), 11-12; R. Baxter, *A Key for Catholicks* (1659), 328-30.

120. S. Clarke, *Golden Apples* (1659), 38, 47, 62, 84, 87, 150-1; J. Browne, *History of Congregationalism . . . in Norfolk and Suffolk* (1877), 225; Morrill, *Cheshire*, 269; R. Howell, *Newcastle-upon-Tyne and the Puritan Revolution* (Oxford, 1967), 246-7; Underdown, *Somerset*, 188.

121. *Diary of Sir Archibald Johnston*, 134-5; *Letters and Journals of Robert Baillie*, iii. 429; Dr Williams's Library, MS. 59, iii, fol. 185; v, fols 48, 136; R. Hubberthorne [and E. Burrough], *An Answer to a Declaration* (1659), 20-22.

122. *The Interest of England stated* (1659), 15. See also *An Apologie*

for the Royal Party (1659); *Calendar of State Papers and Manuscripts Relating to English Affairs . . . Venice* (1931), xxxii (1659-1661), 91.

123.   GBS, i. 516; W. Kennett, *A Register and Chronicle* (1728), 92.

124.   W. Prynne, *A Brief Necessary Vindication* (1659), frontispiece; *The Autobiography of Mrs Alice Thornton* (Surtees Soc., lxii, 1875), 100; L. Hutchinson, *Memoirs of the Life of Colonel Hutchinson* (1968), 317.

125.   Worcester College Library, Clark MS. 32, fol. 41; *Several Letters from the Lord General Monck* (1660), 37; J. Price, *The Mystery and Method of his Majesty's Happy Restauration* (1680), 31.

126.   Davies, *Restoration*, 162-4; *Information from some Souldiers* (Edinburgh, 1659), printed in G. Davies, *The Early History of the Coldstream Guards* (Oxford, 1924), 135-6; *Calendar of the Clarendon State Papers*, ed. F. J. Routledge (Oxford, 1932), iv. 516; Price, *Mystery and Method*, 32.

127.   G. Willington, *The Thrice Welcome and Happy Inauguration* (1660), 4-5.

128.   FHL, Swarthmore MS. v. 93.

129.   *Iter Boreale* (1660), 5. A manuscript note in the Bodleian Library's copy, Wood 465(5), attributes it to Robert Wilde.

130.   For Fairfax's rising, see A. H. Woolrych, 'Yorkshire and the Restoration', *Yorkshire Archaeological Journal*, xxxix (1956-8).

131.   *The Monckton Papers* (Misc. Philob. Soc. xv, 1884), 26, 27, 29, 86; *HMC Fifth Report* (1876), 193-4; *An Extract of a Letter from York* (1659).

132.   Davies, *Restoration*, 248ff.; *A Sober Vindication* (1660), printed in *Memoirs of Edmund Ludlow*, ii. 473-6; *Mercurius Politicus*, 603 (12-19 Jan. 1659/60), [1030-31]; G. Pressick, *A breife Relation* [Dublin, 1660]; *The Declaration of the Army in Ireland* (1659), 1; FHL, Swarthmore MS. i. 318.

133.   E.g. *The Humble Address, and hearty Desires of the Gentlemen . . . of Northampton* (1660); *The Humble desires of the Knights,*

Gentlemen . . . of Leicester (1659); *CSP, 1659-60*, 340.
However, petitions from Gloucester, Cornwall, Berks.,
Norfolk, Bucks., Kent, Warwick, and Oxford did not mention
the sects (though some talked in terms of divisions in the church
and the dangers that religion had faced). For the petitions, see
BL, 669 f23.

134.   *A Curtain-Conference* [1660]; *To the Supreme Authority . . .
An Humble Petition on the behalf of many Thousands of
Quakers, Fifth-Monarchy men, Anabaptists, &c.* (1660); *To the
Right Honourable . . . Parliament* (1660); *A Declaration of Old
Nick* [1660]; *Democritus Turned Statesman* (1659); *Fanatique
Queries* (1660); *The Acts and Monuments of the Late Rump*
(1660).

135.   *A Letter from Shrewsbury* (1660).

136.   *The Diary of Samuel Pepys*, ed. R. Latham and W. Matthews
(1970), i. 111; *Mercurius Civicus*, 2 (17-24 April 1660), 13-16;
Clarendon MS. 71, fols 234, 272, 343.

137.   For the attitude of the Quakers towards Lambert, see FHL,
Portfolio MS. i. 54; Historical Society of Pennsylvania, Etting
MS. iv. 2.

138.   Morrill, *Cheshire*, 326.

139.   Norfolk RO, Norwich Mayors' Court Book 1654-1666, fol.
116v.

140.   Friends' Meeting House, York, MS. 36, pt ii, pp. 2-3.

141.   See Bodleian Library, Carte MS. 73, fols 402-4.

142.   For Wales: GBS, ii, Wales, 18; Besse, i. 742; FHL, Swarthmore
MS. iv. 252; National Library of Wales, MS. 11440 D, fol. 43;
Lewis and others, *For the King*, 5. For London: *Diary of
Samuel Pepys*, i. 44; FHL, Swarthmore MSS. v. 93, iv. 261;
GBS, ii, London, 4; *Mercurius Politicus*, 612 (15-22 March
1659/60), 1183; T. Salthouse and others, *To both the Houses of
Parliament* (1660).

143.   T. C. Barnard, *Cromwellian Ireland* (Oxford, 1975), 133;
Besse, ii. 464; FHL, Swarthmore MS. iv. 238; Society of
Friends Historical Library, Dublin, MS. B 20, pp. 2-5.

144.   FHL, Swarthmore MS. iv. 134, i. 169; Somerset RO, DD/SFR
       8/1, pt i, fol. 37v; GBS, i. 106-7, 345-6; Spufford, *Contrasting
       Communities*, 290; Dorset RO, N10/A15, 1, 2; G. Fox the
       younger, *A True Relation* (1660), 3.

145.   Reynolds and others, *Seasonable Exhortation*, 3-12; Baxter,
       Right Rejoycing, 45-7.

146.   Willington, *Thrice Welcome and Happy Inauguration*, 6.

147.   E. Reynolds, *The Author and Subject of Healing* (1660), 27;
       J. G[askin], *A Just Defence* (1660), introductory epistle; R.
       South, *Ecclesiasticall Policy* (Oxford, 1660), 23.

148.   W. Brownsword, *England's Grounds of Joy*, quoted in F.
       Nicholson and E. Axon, *The Older Nonconformity in Kendal*
       (Kendal, 1915), 70.

149.   See R. Clifton, 'The Popular Fear of Catholics during the
       English Revolution', *P. and P.*, 52 (1971); B. Manning, *The
       English People and the English Revolution* (1976), ch. 2; G.
       Lefebvre, *The Great Fear of 1789* (NY, 1973).

150.   FHL, Swarthmore MS. iii. 145.

6 THE TRANSFORMATION OF QUAKERISM

1.   FHL, 'Some Account of the Birth Education . . . of Josiah
       Langdale' (1723), 1-3. The quotations from Langdale appear by
       permission of the Library Committee of the Religious Society
       of Friends.

2.   Ibid, 6-8.

3.   Ibid, 8, 10-11.

4.   Ibid, 12-15.

5.   See p. 9 above.

6.   FHL, 'Some Account of . . . Josiah Langdale', 12-13.

7.   Ibid, 15, 17.

8.   W. Kennett, *A Register and Chronicle* (1728), 582.

9. G. Fox the younger, *A Noble Salutation* (1660), 13.

10. PRO, SP 29/21/107.

11. Besse, i. 167-8.

12. GBS, i. 19.

13. FHL, Portfolio MS. i. 48.

14. Hampshire RO, 24M54/15, fols 6v ff.

15. GBS, i. 424.

16. PRO, SP29/19/18; *Journals of the House of Commons*, viii. 39; Besse, i. 195.

17. Cheshire RO, QJB/11a, fol. 8v; GBS, i. 560.

18. See B. Reay, 'The Authorities and Early Restoration Quakerism', *JEH*, xxxiv (1983), 72-3.

19. *The History of the Life of Thomas Ellwood* (1714), 101; FHL, Portfolio MS. i. 20.

20. For the above in more detail, see Reay, 'Authorities and Early Restoration Quakerism', 75-84; C. Horle, 'Judicial encounters with Quakers 1660-1688', *JFHS*, liv (1977).

21. Braithwaite, *Second Period*, 98, n.2.

22. Cole, 'Quakers and Politics', chs 8-9.

23. FHL, Edmond Crosse MS., pp. 2-3.

24. See BL, Add. MS. 36735, pp. 24-5; and FHL, Charles Lloyd MS. 62/11.

25. E. B[urrough], *A Visitation and Presentation* (1660), 10-11.

26. *A Declaration from the Harmles & Innocent People of God* (1660), 4, 8.

27. F. B. Tolles, *Quakers and the Atlantic Culture* (NY, 1960), 52.

28. Tolles, *Quakers*, 49; J. M. Chu, 'The Social and Political Contexts of Heterodoxy: Quakerism in Seventeenth-Century Kittery', *New England Quarterly*, liv (1981); D. W. Jordan, ' "God's Candle" within Government: Quakers and Politics in Early Maryland', *William and Mary Quarterly*, xxxix (1982).

29. A. Lloyd, *Quaker Social History* (1950), 83, 90-1; Braithwaite, *Second Period*, 95, 98, 112; R. Clark, ' "The Gangreen of Quakerism": An Anti-Quaker Anglican Offensive in England after the Glorious Revolution', *JRH*, xi (1981), 413-14.

30. Cambridge University Library, EDR E20.

31. [R. Rich], *Hidden Things brought to Light* (1678), 28.

32. Historical Society of Pennsylvania, Etting MS. iv. 2.

33. PRO, Assi 45/7/2/172.

34. Vann, *Social Development*, 16-17.

35. *Adventures by Sea of Edward Coxere*, ed. E. H. W. Meyerstein (Oxford, 1945), 87, 89, 102. See also *A Short Account of the Life of Mr John Pennyman* (1703), 18-19; Medical Society of London, 'Transcripts of John Ward's Diary 1648-1679', v. 1122.

36. PRO, SP 29/63/70; C. Leslie, *The Snake in the Grass* (1698), 224-5.

37. J. P[ennyman], *The Quakers Unmask'd* (1691), 1-2.

38. G. Fox the younger, *A Collection of the several Books* (1665), 262-3; PRO, PC 2/55, pp. 96-7; FHL, Spence MS. iii.2.

39. Reay, 'Early Quaker Activity', 182-8.

40. J. R. Jacob, *Henry Stubbe, radical Protestantism and the early Enlightenment* (Cambridge, 1983), 6, and *passim*.

41. FHL, Edmond Crosse MS., pp. 55-6.

42. FHL, Charles Lloyd MS. 62/13.

43. Reay, 'Early Quaker Activity', 188.

44.   Quoted in F. B. Tolles, *Meeting House and Counting House* (NY, 1963), 111.

45.   Ibid, 111-12.

46.   G. B. Nash, *Quakers and Politics* (Princeton, 1968), 31-2; J. E. Pomfret, *The Province of West New Jersey 1609-1702* (Princeton, 1956), 93-8.

47.   Nash, *Quakers and Politics*, 39-43; M. B. Endy, *William Penn and Early Quakerism* (Princeton, 1973), 361.

48.   T. O'Malley, ' "Defying the Powers and Tempering the Spirit". A Review of Quaker Control over their Publications 1672-1689', *JEH*, xxxiii (1982).

49.   FHL, MS. Morning Meeting Minutes 1673-1692, pp. 5, 60, 122.

50.   O'Malley, ' "Defying the Powers" ', 87.

51.   See D. Runyon, 'Types of Quaker Writings by Year – 1650-1699', in *Early Quaker Writings*, ed. H. Barbour and A. Roberts (Grand Rapids, 1973), 567-76.

52.   FHL, MS. Morning Meeting Minutes 1673-1692, pp. 4, 69.

53.   Cf. Endy, *William Penn*; P. M. Oliver, 'Quaker Testimony and the Lamb's War' (Univ. of Melbourne Ph.D. thesis, 1977).

54.   H. Forde, 'Derbyshire Quakers 1650-1761' (Univ. of Leicester Ph.D. thesis, 1977), ch. 7, p. 217.

55.   J. Butler, ' "Gospel Order Improved": The Keithian Schism and the Exercise of Quaker Ministerial Authority in Pennsylvania', *William and Mary Quarterly*, xxxi (1974), 434, 436.

56.   Oliver, 'Quaker Testimony', 246.

57.   Butler, ' "Gospel Order Improved" ', 446.

58.   *A Brief Relation* (1662), 5; Clark, ' "Gangrene of Quakerism" ', 407.

59.   E. K. L. Quine, 'The Quakers in Leicestershire 1648-1780'

(Univ. of Nottinghamshire Ph.D. thesis, 1968), 153-4; S. H. G. Fitch, *Colchester Quakers* (Colchester, 1963?), 42.

60.   *JGF*, i., introduction.

61.   See FHL, tract volume 268, for the original with the manuscript alterations made by Whitehead when he was preparing reprints in 1703.

62.   Vann, *Social Development*, 125.

63.   Lloyd, *Quaker Social History*, 129-31; Butler, ' "Gospel Order Improved" ', 441. H. Lidbetter, 'Quaker Meeting Houses, 1670-1850', *Architectural Review*, xcix (1946).

64.   R. Bauman, *Let your words be few* (Cambridge, 1983), ch. 9, esp. p. 149.

65.   W. Crouch, *Posthuma Christiana* (1712), 26; Cambridgeshire RO, R59/25/1/1, 6 Oct. 1691.

66.   Quine, 'Quakers in Leicestershire', 154; Fitch, *Colchester Quakers*, 45.

67.   Lloyd, *Quaker Social History, passim*; Braithwaite, *Second Period*, chs 9-10.

68.   J. F. McGregor, 'The Baptists: Fount of all Heresy', in McGregor and B. Reay (eds), *Radical Religion in the English Revolution* (Oxford, 1984), 34, 39, 43; also M. Mullett, *Radical Religious Movements in Early Modern Europe* (1980), 67-8.

69.   J. W. Frost, *The Quaker Family in Colonial America* (NY, 1973), 83-6.

70.   R. H. Evans, 'The Quakers of Leicestershire 1660-1714', *Transactions of the Leicestershire Archaeological Society*, xxviii (1952), 73.

71.   Vann, *Social Development*, 98, 116-21.

72.   FHL, Portfolio MS. xxxiii. 104: 'it is an evill wind, wch ariseth from ye airy Spirit'.

73.   Frost, *Quaker Family*, 53-4, 56-7; Devon RO, 874D/M155.

See, for example, Cambridgeshire RO, R59/25/1/2: local meetings reporting back to the Huntingdonshire Quarterly Meeting: 'Downham, pretty well', 'Balsham, Things pretty well'.

74. *SQM*, 80.

75. Ibid, 74, 83.

76. *The First Minute Book of the Gainsborough Monthly Meeting of the Society of Friends 1669-1689* (Lincoln Rec. Soc., xxxviii, 1948), 66.

77. *MMB(2)*, 6.

78. E.g. Ibid, 10, 13, 35-6, 86, 100, 120, 167; Somerset RO, DD/SFR W, pp. 30, 33, 133; *Minute Book of the Gainsborough Monthly Meeting . . . 1669-1689*, 58-9, 61, 66-7, 74-5, 87 (trees), 102.

79. Cambridgeshire RO, R59/25/1/1, 3 Feb. 1674, 14 Nov. 1682; *MMB(1)*, 113; *MMB(2)*, xxi, 39, 69, 70, 202.

80. The Bristol records suggest an interval of nine months; the Huntingdonshire records suggest longer. *MMB(2)*, 45, 48-9, 63, 68; Cambridgeshire RO, R59/25/1/1, 3 Feb. 1675, 4 Feb. 1678, 6 July 1697.

81. Forde, 'Derbyshire Quakers', 140. For some examples of discouragement: *SQM*, 90, 148, 207; Cambridgeshire RO, R59/25/1/1, 6 Jan. 1674; *MMB(2)*, 22, 66.

82. FHL, MS. Six Weeks' Meeting Minutes 1671-1682, p. 9; *SQM*, 182. For some examples, see: *SQM*, 81, 93, 106, 116, 124, 148, 180, 213, 215, 229; Wiltshire RO, WRO 1699/19, pp. 9, 25, 29-30, 201; Cambridgeshire RO, R59/25/1/2, 2 Sept. 1679, 7 Dec. 1680, 3 June 1684; R59/25/1/1, 1 Oct. 1678, 1 Feb. 1681.

83. *MMB(2)*, 50, 67; Cambridgeshire RO, R59/25/1/1, 8 Aug. 1682, 9 Jan. 1683; Somerset RO, DD/SFR W, p. 10; *SQM*, 76.

84. *SQM*, 130-1, 166-7.

85. Wiltshire RO, WRO 1699/19, pp. 142, 144, 149, 151, 157, 158, 161.

86.   *MMB(1)*, 19.

87.   Cambridgeshire RO, R59/25/1/1, 6 April 1680.

88.   Wiltshire RO, WRO 1699/19, p. 13.

89.   Vann, *Social Development*, 137.

90.   Somerset RO, DD/SFR 10/2/49; DD/SFR 10/1/45.

91.   Somerset RO, DD/SFR W, p. 73; FHL, MS. Six Weeks'
       Meeting Minutes 1671-1682, p. 22.

92.   E.g. Cambridgeshire RO, R59/25/1/1, 4 Jan. 1675;
       R59/25/1/5, 6 Sept. 1676, *et seq.*

93.   Wiltshire RO, WRO 1699/19, p. 3; *SQM*, 205.

94.   For Weber, see A. Giddens, *Capitalism and modern social
       theory* (Cambridge, 1978), ch. 9; M. Weber, *The Protestant
       Ethic and the Spirit of Capitalism* (1976), *passim*.

95.   J. Parnell, *A Shield of the Truth* (1655), 2-3.

96.   T. Adams and R. Farnworth, *An Easter-Reckoning* (1656), 25,
       28.

97.   N. Smith, *The Quakers Spiritual Court* [1668], 35-8.

98.   *MMB(1)*, 4, 108; *MMB(2)*, 109, 110-12, 115, 152.

99.   Somerset RO, DD/SFR W, *passim* (for Petheram), 8, 12, 15,
       125, 135.

100.   Berkshire RO, D/F 2A 1/1, no pagination.

101.   Cf. K. Wrightson, 'The Puritan Reformation of Manners'
       (Univ. of Cambridge Ph.D. thesis, 1973).

102.   *MMB(1)*, 11, 15, 21; *MMB(2)*, 41, 153, 157; *SQM*, 33, 75, 81,
       90, 98, 102, 148; Somerset RO, DD/SFR W, pp. 56, 141;
       Cambridgeshire RO, R59/25/1/1, 1 Oct. 1678.

103.   Derbyshire Quarterly Meeting, 1682, quoted in Forde,
       'Derbyshire Quakers', 134.

104.   William Penn, quoted in Tolles, *Quakers*, 80.

105.   Crouch, *Posthuma Christiana*, 136-7.

106.   *JGF*, ii. 428.

107.   T. Simmons, *The Voice of the Just Uttered* (1657), 4; *An Account of Many Remarkable Passages of the Life of Oliver Sansom* (1710), 7; FHL, 'Some Account of . . . Josiah Langdale', 1.

108.   *JGF*, ii. 476.

109.   T. Hart, *The Foundation* (1659).

110.   H. E. Rollins (ed.), *Cavalier and Puritan* (NY, 1923), 68-9.

111.   P. Gregg, *Free-Born John* (1961), 347.

112.   L. Wright, *The Literary Life of the Early Friends 1650-1725* (NY, 1966), 24, 57.

113.   Braithwaite, *Second Period*, 507, 510, 511-14; Tolles, *Quakers*, ch. 5.

114.   *MMB(1)*, 26-7, 36-8.

115.   See Tolles, *Quakers*, 130, and examples between pp. 62-3.

116.   *JGF*, i. 396-7; Braithwaite, *Beginnings*, 45-6.

117.   Devon RO, 874 D/Q7; Tolles, *Quakers*, 120. See also Braithwaite, *Second Period*, 511-14; Lloyd, *Quaker Social History*, 73.

118.   Tolles, *Quakers*, 88.

119.   B. Reay, 'Quaker Opposition to Tithes 1652-1660', *P. and P.*, 86 (1980), 118-20.

120.   Clark, ' "Gangreen of Quakerism" ', 410.

121.   R. Porter, 'Being Mad in Georgian England', *History Today*, 31 (Dec. 1981), 44.

122. K. L. Carroll, 'Quaker Weavers at Newport, Ireland', *JFHS*, liv (1976), 15-16.

123. Vann, *Social Development*, 200-1.

124. Braithwaite, *Second Period*, 237.

125. *JGF*, ii. 461.

126. Barbour, *Quakers*, 230; Braithwaite, *Second Period*, 260.

Index